DATE DUE			

CONGREGATIONS
IN CONFLICT

KEITH HARTMAN

CONGREGATIONS IN CONFLICT

The Battle over Homosexuality

RUTGERS UNIVERSITY PRESS
New Brunswick, New Jersey

Copyright © 1996 by Keith Hartman
Published by Rutgers University Press, New Brunswick, New Jersey
Manufactured in the United States of America

Library of Congress Cataloging-in-Publication Data
Hartman, Keith, 1966–
Congregations in conflict : the battle over homosexuality
/ Keith Hartman.
p. cm.
Includes bibliographical references and index.
ISBN 0-8135-2229-3
1. Homosexuality—Religious aspects—Christianity.
2. Gay men—United States—Religious life.
3. Lesbians—United States—Religious life.
4. Church controversies.
I. Title.
BR115.H6H38   1996
261.8'35766'0973—dc20   95-8754   CIP

British Cataloging-in-Publication information available

To Jim, who read my drafts, edited my prose, corrected my mistakes, gave me much good business advice, and remembered to feed the cat when I was too engrossed in writing. Both of us are glad you were around.

Contents

Preface

A Methodist church puts it minister on trial for marching in a gay rights parade. A Quaker meeting struggles with a marriage request from two lesbians. A Baptist church debates the ordination of a gay divinity student, and is thrown out of the Southern Baptist Convention for deciding to go ahead with it. In churches across the country, a fascinating and bitter conflict is being played out.

Homosexuality is the most divisive element facing the Church today. Like the issue of slavery a century and a half ago, it is a matter that stirs up passionate convictions, one that threatens to turn members of the same faith against one another, to divide churches, and even to split denominations. Like slavery, it is an issue that calls up basic questions about what it means to be a Christian: How does one know right from wrong? Is the Bible infallible? To what extent does the Church reflect God's will, and to what extent does it reflect the traditions of society? Do good Christians always follow the Church's teachings, or are they allowed to think for themselves on moral issues? And to what sources does one finally look to determine what God wants?

This book began in 1992, when I was a graduate student at Duke University. One of my good friends was John Blevins, a Divinity School student whom I had met through Duke's gay and lesbian group. John had been helping me track down biblical references for a column called "Sex, God, etc." I wrote in the school newspaper. I had gotten into a friendly debate with some fundamentalist letter-writers, and I wanted to make sure they were playing fair with their use of Scripture. One evening, I was splitting a pizza with John's boyfriend, Reggie, and happened to ask when John would be home. Reggie groaned and made some comment about having

become a "Binkley Widow." Having no idea what he was talking about,
I asked Reggie to explain. As a result I stumbled headfirst into a remarkable story.

John was in his final year of divinity school, and was ready to begin the
process of being ordained as a Southern Baptist minister. Accordingly, he
had gone before the Board of Deacons at Olin T. Binkley Memorial Baptist,
the church to which he belonged, and asked to be licensed as a candidate
to preach the gospel. Several of the deacons already knew that John was
gay—he had never made much of a secret of it—and John made a point
of informing the rest of them, so that they would know what they were
getting into. This left the church leadership in a quandary: while some of
them felt that homosexuals as a group should not be ordained, others felt
that John as an individual would make a fine minister.

The deacons' response to this problem was novel. They admitted that
they didn't know the right thing to do, and they called upon the congregation of Binkley to help them decide. For several months, the members
of Binkley had studied the matter: analyzing Scripture, reading up on scientific theories of sexuality, grappling with the differences between valid
tradition and simple prejudice, debating the issues, and trying to help
each other find the truth. It was something that I had never seen a church
do before. The denomination I had been raised in operated on the principle
that no one could ever question the church's teachings or its traditions.
The church was so sure of its own infallibility, so sure that it had a monopoly
on the truth, that it considered any free thought to be blasphemy. This
attitude had been one of my prime reasons for dropping out of the church
as a teenager. And perhaps it also explains why the situation at Binkley fas-
cinated me so much—here was a church that was actually encouraging its
members to question their traditions, to think for themselves about what
was morally right, to go out looking for the truth rather than smugly
assuming that they already knew it.

Noticing my interest in his story, John invited me to attend one of the
church meetings at which the congregation would be questioning him
about his own beliefs on the Bible, sexuality, and the ministry. I went,
and from that evening on I was hooked. The drama was irresistible. Both
sides were honestly convinced that they were acting in the name of God.
These were people with violently opposed convictions, who were nonetheless bound together in a community of faith. How could they ever resolve
such an issue? How could people with such extreme points of view reach

one another, change one another? With appeals to logic? To fair play? Or by more personal means?

I eventually wound up covering the story for several magazines, some of them in the Christian press, some of them gay and lesbian publications. In the course of researching the articles, I quickly discovered that I was onto something larger. Binkley was not an isolated incident. My interviews with that congregation had alerted me to conflicts at two other churches, Pullen Baptist and Fairmont Methodist, and through other channels I learned of a debate going on at a Quaker meeting. There was definitely a story to be told here. The only question was how to tell it.

I briefly considered conducting a broad study, in which I would choose cases from across the country. This would give me plenty of churches to pick from, and I would probably be able to find a representative case from every major denomination. I quickly decided, however, that I would miss much of the real story with such a broad focus. One of the things that had intrigued me early on was the interaction among local churches. Members of Binkley would talk about conflicts at other churches, and how they had been resolved. Ministers would watch how their colleagues handled a crisis, and learn from their mistakes. Losers in the conflict at one church would quit it in disgust, only to turn up as key players in another congregation's fight. The ways in which these churches affected one another, sometimes unintentionally, were critical to understanding what each of them had experienced. I realized that it would be impossible to tell the story of any one church by itself. I needed to tell the story of a whole community.

In the end I chose to concentrate on a group of nine churches centered in the Research Triangle area of North Carolina. The Triangle includes the cities of Raleigh, Durham, and Chapel Hill. It is something of a melting pot: surrounded by tobacco fields, it also contains three major universities and is home to a variety of immigrants from other regions of the United States who have come to work in the growing high-tech industry. It is an interesting area where, geography aside, the Bible Belt seems to intersect the Northeast and the West Coast.

The narrow focus did create a few problems. Regrettably, I was never able to locate a nearby Jewish congregation that was grappling with the issue of homosexuality. (Although I did learn of several cases in which rabbis had performed same-sex weddings, they were all in other parts of the country.) Similarly, circumstances forced me to omit several mainline Protestant denominations. Although I did locate interesting struggles at a Lutheran and a Presbyterian church, neither turned out to be suitable for publication.

That said, I did have the privilege of watching a group of fascinating stories unfold: how one Southern Baptist congregation decided to marry two gay men. Why a Black Catholic church expelled its gay and lesbian group as part of an effort to be more "inclusive." How a conservative Seventh Day Adventist became the first straight minister of a gay denomination. What happened when an entire order of aging celibate monks began coming out of the closet. How an Episcopal priest decided to bless a lesbian relationship, and why a closeted gay man led the charge to fire him for it.

These struggles are interesting not only because they show how people form and change their opinions about homosexuality, but because they show how different religious traditions deal with conflict: from the grass-roots "priesthood of the believer" doctrine of the Baptists to the hierarchical approach of the Roman Catholics, from the avoidance mechanisms of the Methodists to the "clearness process" of the Quakers. How a denomination handles its internal disputes says a great deal about the true nature of its faith.

I have incurred many debts in the course of this project. In particular, I would like to thank the Durham Arts Council, which provided an Emerging Artist Grant to help fund my research. All photographs in the book were lent by their subjects or taken by myself. I would also like to thank Leslie Mitchner and Professor James D. Woods for their useful comments and suggestions. Rob Odom was a fountain of good advice on dealing with agents, publishers, and contracts. A special thanks to my editor, Elizabeth Gretz, who was a pleasant surprise indeed. My previous relations with editors have often been a bit stormy—it seems as if I've written one story and they are trying to edit it into something completely different. Elizabeth, however, always seemed to have a clear grasp of what I was trying to do. Rather than redirecting my work, her editing refined and clarified it.

Last, I would like to thank all the people who opened up their private lives and agreed to be interviewed for this book. I have done my best to accurately depict their actions and ideas in the following pages, no matter which side of the various conflicts they were on. It is my belief that we can respect each other, even if we cannot always agree with each other.

CONGREGATIONS IN CONFLICT

CHAPTER 1

The Generation Gap:
Fairmont Methodist

When Jimmy Creech was a young man, he heard about three civil rights
workers who had been murdered in Mississippi. "It's their own fault," his
father had told him. "They shouldn't have gone down there in the first
place."

Years later, Jimmy would tell a reporter for the *Independent Weekly*
that it was a moment which had opened his eyes. "It was like I finally
understood the evil that good people can do. My father was saying that
there was a way of life in the South that should not be challenged. And
I realized that for some people, maintaining order is more important than
injustice."[1]

Warsaw, North Carolina, 1984. The Reverend Jimmy Creech had never
thought much about homosexuality. Oh, he'd wondered about it, in the
offhand sort of way that one wonders about the Bermuda Triangle, or
Bigfoot, or any other mystery that one never really expects to understand. Why would a man want to have sex with another man? And how
could two women even have sex without a man present?

Like most of the congregation of his Methodist church, Reverend
Creech assumed that he had never met a homosexual. And like most of
his congregation, he was wrong.

Nineteen eighty-four was the year that the General Conference of the
United Methodist Church codified the denomination's position on

homosexuality. The gay rights movement was becoming increasingly visible, and the Methodists decided to take a strong stand against it. The members of the conference voted to add a statement to the Methodists' *Book of Discipline* stating that the practice of homosexuality is "incompatible with Christian teaching" and forbidding any homosexual from becoming a minister in the church.

Now, a week after that meeting, one of Reverend Creech's charges had come to resign his membership in the church. It was a man whom Jimmy had known for several years—one of those active members who form the backbone of any congregation, the kind of guy whom you could always count on when the church needed a volunteer to put in work on something. Stunned, Jimmy asked the man why he was leaving.

"Because I won't be a part of a church that condemns me."

Methodist ministers don't spend more than a few years at any one church, and in 1987 Bishop C. P. Minnick assigned Jimmy Creech to a new parish, Fairmont United Methodist Church, in downtown Raleigh, North Carolina.

Fairmont was a church with unique problems. About fifteen years earlier, there had been a bitter generational split over control of the church. The younger members, who had been attending for five years or so, had wanted to begin taking on some of the responsibility for running the church. The older members, however, felt that they had invested too much of their lives in Fairmont to ever turn over control. They were the ones who had built Fairmont, and they felt entitled to run it. The older generation effectively locked the younger members out of the key committees that managed the affairs of the church. The younger generation had responded by leaving.

Fairmont's congregation grew smaller and older—two warning signs that a church is not likely to survive much longer. Indeed, Fairmont had seemed close to dying when Eric Carson had been brought in as minister. A passionate man from Northern Ireland, Carson worked hard to bring in new members. At his insistence, Fairmont began hosting the Wesley Fellowship, the Methodist campus ministry for North Carolina State. This brought in a number of young people, many of whom became members and stayed with the church after graduation.

The church that Creech inherited from Carson still bore certain scars from the old conflict—most noticeably the lack of members between the ages of thirty-five and fifty-five. There were young couples with small children, and there were retired members with grandchildren, but there were none of the middle-aged couples with teenagers that can sometimes serve to bridge the two groups. Still, a compromise had been reached, and the younger members were slowly being accepted into leadership positions. By and large, things seemed to be going well.

Jimmy Creech arrived at his new church in June of 1987. He had been described to the church as a young and energetic minister, a "rising star" in the North Carolina Methodist Conference.[2] In his first meeting with Fairmont's Pastor-Parish Relations Committee, Reverend Creech said that he felt a calling to be involved in the community, and that he planned to work actively on social justice issues. He talked about his principal interest at the time, human rights abuses in Central America, and about his hope to go to Central America as part of the Witness for Peace program. He concluded by saying that a good minister sometimes has to challenge his congregation.

Jimmy did so quickly, with sermons on civil rights, Central America, homelessness, and the responsibility of the church to involve itself in the world and deal with social problems. This liberal theology upset many older members of Fairmont, who had grown used to Carson's preaching style—more about personal salvation, less about the ills of society. The older members also complained that Jimmy was too "hands on" in his management style, that he was trying to take power away from their committees. They pointed out, quite correctly, that Methodist ministers come and go, but the congregation is with the church for life. As they saw it, the church should be run by its members, not some minister who would only be around for four or five years.

But such complaints were only background grumblings. It takes time for any congregation to adapt to a new minister and vice versa. Most people viewed these problems as nothing more than growing pains.

Reverend Creech happened to arrive in Raleigh at the same time that the city's Commission on Human Resources and Human Relations was debating a change to Raleigh's nondiscrimination statute. Nancy Kepple, a member of the commission, had proposed that the statute be expanded to include sexual orientation. If passed, the measure would mean that employees of the city government could no longer be fired or demoted simply for being gay. Although many racial and religious minorities already enjoyed such protection in Raleigh, there were some on the city council who argued that homosexuals didn't need it.

To Kepple such words had a familiar ring. She had lived through the desegregation of North Carolina, and remembered hearing those same arguments applied to blacks. In their case too the real question, "Do they *deserve* basic protection under the law?" had been replaced with the more debatable, "Do they really *need* this protection?"

For several weeks Kepple had been discussing the matter with the Reverend Jim Lewis, an Episcopal priest. It seemed to Lewis that there were a number of local clergy who were sympathetic to gay demands for equal protection. The problem was that none of them ever spoke out on the subject, so the issue was being dominated by the fundamentalists, who were always talking about homosexuals and opposed any rights for them. From the outside, it must look as if the Church was monolithic in its stand condemning homosexuals.

Kepple knew that no city council member would be willing to take on the entire Church. She would have to show them that they were only taking on one part of it. An open hearing was coming up, when people on both sides of the issue could speak their piece to the city council. When she was rounding up speakers to support the measure, Kepple made a special point of inviting members of the clergy.

The hearing was supposed to be the gay and lesbian community's chance to prove that it did indeed need protection. And although the testimony of its members failed to persuade Mayor Avery Upchurch, it did convince the rest of the city council, who passed the measure over his objection. The testimony also made quite an impact on the ministers and priests who had come. Person after person stood up and spoke of being beaten, black-mailed, fired from their jobs, and harassed by police. A man spoke of being knifed, and several women talked about losing custody of their children. One gay man even described being driven out to a cornfield and shot in the back.

But what really shocked the ministers was the way that these people spoke about the Church. For them, the Church was not a source of strength and safety, but one of the forces out to persecute them—which was very disturbing for the clergy to hear. The ministers had always thought of Christ as a source of love, as a champion of the underdog. To hear that His name had been used to justify violence was deeply troubling.

After the hearing, a few of the clergy got together to compare what they knew about homosexuals and to figure out how the Church should be ministering to these people. They met several more times, and eventually became the core of a discussion group on homosexuality and the Church.

That September a vigil for peace in Central America was held in downtown Raleigh. Reverend Creech attended, and he happened to strike up a conversation with Nancy Kepple. Her son had been kidnapped by the U.S.-backed Contras, but had eventually been released unharmed. Their conversation wandered from U.S. foreign policy to civil rights and eventually to local politics. Nancy was shocked to learn that Jimmy knew nothing about that summer's debate over the nondiscrimination statute. They talked about the measure for some time, and Nancy told Jimmy about the clergy discussion group. Intrigued, he agreed to come to their next meeting.

By this time the original group had added several members, including a Roman Catholic priest, a Lutheran pastor, and a rabbi. The group had also moved beyond purely theoretical discussions. The members were now talking about specific actions they could take to counter the message of hate coming from so many churches and to promote a more charitable, more Christian understanding of homosexuality. Jimmy, with his belief that the church should be on the front lines of the struggle for social justice rather than dragging its heels, felt right at home.

"We began to talk about what we could do," recalls Creech. "We needed to sit down and talk to each other and understand. We needed to create a situation where lesbians, gay men, and straight people could talk to one another and understand what their life experiences were like.

"Our principal concern was that the Christian gospel was a statement of God's grace, and not of judgment. And that justice was a standard by which we should judge how the Church behaved. The Church had to be held accountable for its injustices. So we decided that we would have a conference the following spring, to which we would invite people to sit and share stories. We would also invite someone from the Divinity School at Duke to come and deal with biblical issues, since the Bible seemed to be a major focus for those who were so strong in their opposition, so hostile to gay men and lesbians."

About ninety people attended that first conference. "We spent a lot of time listening to each other's stories," remembers Creech. "Many of the gay men and lesbians talked about how significant it was for them to be in a church building and feel safe. That was a new experience.

"It was after that conference that we sort of recognized that there was a need that we had discovered. And that there was in that need a mission."

By now the group had taken the name RRNGLE—the Raleigh Religious Network for Gay and Lesbian Equality. Its initial members had also realized that RRNGLE needed to be an ongoing organization. After some discussion, they decided on a very egalitarian power structure. Rather than having a president or a chairperson, they would simply have a convener, a person who was responsible for calling meetings together. They offered Jimmy the post, and he accepted it. His troubles began that summer.

In June of 1988, the North Carolina Gay and Lesbian Pride Parade was scheduled to be held in Raleigh. Although this annual event is a good deal smaller than similar marches in New York and California, it does provide gays in North Carolina with an important sense of community. It also gives them a chance to stand up and be counted in a state where most are still forced to hide. In addition to intense prejudice, North Carolina still has a "Crimes against Nature" law that has been handed down virtually unchanged from the Court of Henry VIII of England. Although the law is extremely vague, it has been interpreted to outlaw any sexual activity between members of the same sex, even between consenting adults in the privacy of their own home.

As the date of the Pride Parade approached, the members of RRNGLE decided that it was not enough for them just to talk about helping gays and lesbians; it was time for them to take a stand, to make a visible statement of solidarity—to march in the parade. The group knew that the parade was going to provoke heated discussion in local churches, and that not all of it would be charitable. So several weeks ahead of time RRNGLE sent a letter to every member of the clergy in Wake County. For many of the recipients, it was the first time that they had ever heard of the Raleigh Religious Network for Gay and Lesbian Equality.

Dear Colleague,
    Looking at this letterhead you are probably wondering, "What now!

What can I do? Could I support this group?" We have wondered the same and have come together over the past year with common pastoral concerns. You know full well how these times have stretched all of us in the ministry to look at issues that face our congregations, among them being human rights for all people. The issue of homosexuality has knocked at the doors of all religious peoples. . . .

Please be as positive and supportive as you are able. With all the publicity surrounding the June 25th march in Raleigh, please keep in mind the sons and daughters of your congregation who might be there, actually or in spirit. Your response to the media and to your members can keep this particular concern in a pastoral light, exhibiting the compassion that all sons and daughters of God deserve.[3]

The members of RRNGLE were concerned about how the letter should be signed. Any individual whose name appeared on the letter would be sure to draw criticism from the more conservative clergy in the county. Jimmy, however, felt strongly that the letter should be signed by a minister. As he saw it, if the group's members were going to be supportive of gay men and lesbians, then they needed to be "out of the closet" in their support. He also felt that the letter should have a return address and phone number, in case there were any questions. As the group's convener, he signed his own name to the letter and gave the phone number and address of his office at Fairmont.

As the members of RRNGLE had anticipated, a number of clergy in Wake County were not at all happy to hear about this new group of ministers and priests who were supporting civil rights for homosexuals. One minister who was particularly outraged showed the letter to his wife. They both agreed that these people had all taken leave of their senses. After their conversation, the minister's wife photocopied the letter and mailed it anonymously to Charles Holland, an older member of Fairmont United Methodist Church.

As she had expected, Holland was as thoroughly incensed by Creech's behavior as she had been. He further duplicated the letter and circulated copies throughout the Wesley Bible Class, the Sunday school class to which most of the older men belonged. (Unlike the younger generations' classes, the classes for older members were segregated by sex.) For three weeks prior to the Pride Parade, the class talked about nothing but the letter, the threat that homosexuals posed to their church, and how inappropriate it was for Reverend Creech to get involved in something like this.

Strangely enough, during those three weeks not one person from the class actually talked to Reverend Creech about RRNGLE or the parade. Finally, on Friday, the day before the march, a friend in the congregation called Jimmy and asked if he had heard about all the unrest that was brewing. When Jimmy admitted that he hadn't, the friend told him about the discussions that had been going on in the Wesley Bible Class and warned him that the class would be handing him a resolution during the service on Sunday. The resolution condemned anyone who worked or associated with homosexuals.

The next day Creech marched as planned in the Gay and Lesbian Pride Parade. He was genuinely surprised by how much the event moved him.

"It was one of the spiritual highs of my life, to be involved in that march at that time. There is something about having been safely on one side, and then stepping in and being in solidarity with people who are being persecuted. I remember walking in front of the congregation from St. John's Metropolitan Community Church [a gay and lesbian denomination]. There was a man walking along the sidewalk with a twenty-foot cross on his shoulder, and another man walking with a Bible and condemning us all. And all along, St. John's was singing hymns, like 'Just as I Am' and 'Jesus Loves Me, This I Know.' And those hymns had a meaning for me that they had never had before. I knew that I was there for a purpose, and that I was going to remain there."

The next day, during church services, a member of the Wesley Bible Class handed Reverend Creech their resolution:

> The class members believe that in His Scriptures God has made it clear that homosexuality is an abomination in His sight. The class members believe that for Fairmont, or any of its members, or leaders, or any other church to embrace homosexuality, or those who practice it, is an insult to God, that should be strictly avoided, even the appearance of it.
>
> Homosexual persons may have equal rights under man's law as it applies to any human being, but God himself made it clear where they stand in relationship to Him. The Wesley Bible Class wants to clearly uphold the position of the God they worship.[4]

Creech accepted the resolution calmly. During the announcements after worship, he acknowledged that there had been a discussion going on in the church about his ministry to gay men and lesbians. He invited those who wanted to express concerns about this ministry to meet with him in the church that evening.

About thirty people turned up that night. Most of them wanted to ask Reverend Creech about the various biblical prohibitions on homosexual acts, and how he could reconcile these with his ministry to homosexuals. It was a debate that Jimmy was happy to engage in. He talked about his interpretation of the Sodom and Gomorrah story, which he thought had more to do with the rules for hospitality than for sexuality. After all, Lot had appeased the mob by offering them his virgin daughters— hardly a model on which to base one's sexual ethics. Creech talked about the various ancient Greek words that had all been translated as "homosexual" in the King James Bible, and what they had probably meant at the time that the New Testament was written. Based on what little is known of these words, they seem to refer to transvestite prostitutes, not gay men and lesbians in general. And Reverend Creech talked about the ways in which we often use the Bible to justify our prejudices, even as we overlook the verses that would condemn ourselves. For example, why do we still quote the prohibitions on homosexual acts from Leviticus, even though we ourselves violate the other verses of Leviticus by eating shellfish and collecting interest on loans? Is it really that God is so upset by homosexuality, or that we are using God to justify our own discomfort with it?

Creech's main argument, though, was based not on Scripture but on his own personal belief that God was basically fair. Jimmy's conversations with gays at the RRNGLE conference and the Pride Parade had convinced him that, given all the societal prejudice, no one would ever choose to be a homosexual if he could possibly help it. The individuals he had spoken with had fought against being gay, had tried to blend in and be straight, and had slowly realized that they simply weren't put together that way. There was something inside them that they couldn't change. It seemed to Jimmy that some people were just born gay or lesbian, and there was nothing they could do about it. How could a fair God condemn people for being who he'd made them to be?

All in all, Jimmy thought that the meeting had gone well. The crowd had been polite and attentive, and he believed that he had given them good answers to their questions. There had been one awkward moment, when a member of Fairmont had asked him point blank, "Well, since we pay your salary, shouldn't we be able to tell you what you can do?"

That suggestion had really irked Jimmy. "Yes, you pay my salary," he'd responded. "But I'm really accountable to the bishop. And it's up to the bishop to determine whether I stay here or not."

It had been a blunt exchange, but on the whole Jimmy felt that the evening had been very productive. He and the older members had shared opinions, and maybe he'd given them some things to think about.

For their part, the older members thought that Reverend Creech had gone out of his mind. Their pastor's argument about the correct translation of ancient Greek phrases struck them as a legalistic defense of the latest liberal fad. And how could he possibly compare an abomination like homosexuality with the kosher food rules? They were completely different. Homosexuality was just plain wrong. It was obvious, too obvious to even talk about. Of course God frowned on such immorality.

Bill Sharpe, the Methodist campus minister, thinks that the older members were confused by Jimmy's talk of being called to take a stand for justice. "We don't think in our world today in those kinds of terms—of being called to a particular cause, or people. So to them I think that seemed strange. They would interpret it as, 'Well, he's not caring about what's going on in this congregation. All he cares about is the fact that he feels called to that mission.' "

Jimmy himself admits, "I learned later that I didn't really satisfy anybody. That essentially what I did was to confirm their correct belief that I was very much committed to this cause and was not backing off of it."

Indeed, it was after this meeting that the older members of the church made their decision—Creech had to go.

The movement to dispose of Creech began with a visit to the Pastor-Parish Relations Committee (PPRC) by two members of the Wesley Bible Class: George Reynolds and James Stevens, who was a trustee of the church. They told the committee in no uncertain terms that they wanted Creech expelled from Fairmont. They also shared with the Committee their version of what had happened at the Sunday night meeting. Their story was recorded by the PPRC's secretary, along with notes on the speakers:

> The meeting was held with about 33 people present. It had been reported that [Reverend Creech] passed out a flyer with the *Discipline*'s position on homosexuality, and a flyer that announced a meeting on gay rights at Pullen Memorial Baptist Church; that he acknowledged that he was wrong to use the church address and phone number (Stevens notes) and that he said he didn't have to get anyone's permission to use that address because it was his own office and he answered only to the conference (Reynolds); that he was paid by the conference and doesn't have to answer to us (Reynolds) and that he is in charge; that he marched in the demonstration to help homosexuals have pride in their (homosexual) lifestyle; that homosexuals are born that way and can't change; that while he was at Ocracoke he knew that the three top officials in the church were homosexual (Reynolds) (per Reynolds: the church was known to have a lot of homosexuals and that normal people didn't go there); that the church at Warsaw had lots of homosexuals (and per Reynolds: Jimmy must have recruited them there and was doing all of this before he came to Raleigh and must have been supporting homosexuals for 13 or 14 years); when asked what he would do if he had to choose between Fairmont and his ministry he said per Reynolds, 'I don't care what you say or do, I'm going to minister to the homosexuals.' [5]

As before, no one from the class spoke with Jimmy directly. In fact, he was still trying to find ways to work with the more conservative members of his church. The week of the PPRC meeting at which Reynolds and Stevens demanded his removal, Reverend Creech was drafting a letter for Fairmont's newsletter.

> Dear Friends,
>   Since June, there has been a controversy within our church because of my participation in a committee organizing to help the Raleigh community deal with issues related to homosexuality. . . . My purpose, and that of the committee, was to give public witness to the fact that God's love and peace are extended to the homosexual community, just as it is to all of God's people. Because many of you consider homosexuality to be an offense to God, my involvement in the march was confusing, causing some of you to feel betrayed by me.

The *Discipline of the United Methodist Church* states that the Church does not condone the practice of homosexuality and considers the practice of homosexuality to be incompatible with Christian teaching. I affirm and uphold this position. As a United Methodist minister, I am charged by the *Discipline* to offer ministry and guidance to people, including homosexual persons, in their struggles for human fulfillment, as well as spiritual and emotional care. This is a ministry of compassion and reconciliation which neither condones nor condemns homosexual persons, but offers the healing presence of grace. My ministry is not intended to promote or encourage the practice of homosexuality. Instead, it is to respond to the existence of homosexual persons and their need for God's grace. I deeply regret the pain my actions may have caused you. . . .

Another effect of this controversy is the perception that there is a division within the congregation along age lines. Truly this is a misconception. One of the things I am surest of is the mutual love and respect within Fairmont among age groups. We need one another and, I believe, desire to be together. Each of us has gifts to offer one another. Our different perspectives and opinions enrich us.[6]

In retrospect, the last paragraph of the letter would prove the most ironic. When the Pastor-Parish Relations Committee called an open meeting in early July to discuss Jimmy's ministry to homosexuals, it became clear that the congregation was dividing along generational lines. With few exceptions, every member who spoke in support of Reverend Creech came from the younger generation, and everyone who condemned him came from the older.

After the July meeting, the PPRC met with Jimmy to discuss the many things they'd been hearing about him. Committee members sharply criticized him for giving out the church's phone number and address without first asking the committee's permission. By signing Fairmont's address to that letter, they felt that he had made it appear that Fairmont United Methodist Church was taking this controversial stand, not just the Reverend Jimmy Creech as an individual. Jimmy apologized to the committee and agreed to consult with them before doing anything similar in the future.

The committee then questioned Creech in great detail about his ministry to homosexuals. How was it compatible with Scripture? How much time would it require? How much would it interfere with his duties as pastor of Fairmont?

In the end, the PPRC concluded that Jimmy's activities were not contrary to the *Discipline* and would leave him plenty of time for his responsibilities at Fairmont. Furthermore, the committee voted unanimously to send a letter to the congregation supporting Jimmy's special ministry. The letter ended with a statement that Reverend Creech would be happy to meet with any Sunday school classes that wished to discuss his ministry to homosexuals and the issues that it posed to the church.

The Wesley Bible Class took him up on his offer. On Sunday, July 12, Jimmy and three members of the PPRC attended the class. The committee members had decided that they should go along to help smooth things over with the older members and to provide Jimmy with a little moral support in what was likely to be a difficult situation. Later, several members of the class would complain about the PPRC presence. They informed the committee that they had wanted to hear Creech speak for himself, that they had wanted to hear *his* answers to their questions. They pointed out that it was Creech they had invited, not the PPRC.

As before, many of the questions at this meeting centered on scriptural interpretation. However, several people also expressed concern that Creech was sullying Fairmont's good name with his activities. Even if he thought he was acting as a private citizen, everyone would still know that he was their pastor. The members of the class made it very clear that they did not want people thinking that they supported Jimmy in his endeavors to help homosexuals. Still, the class adjourned on a relatively cordial note. As before, however, the civility was deceptive.

Once again, Creech seems to have misunderstood the depth of feeling against his work with the gay community. The meeting had been quite polite—church members discussing a difference of opinion, nothing more. Jimmy believed that people could agree to disagree and leave it at that. The next week, Reverend Creech took his annual vacation, going to Nicaragua as part of the Witness for Peace program.

For their part, the older members were not willing to "agree to disagree." As they saw it, the church exists to tell people what is right and what is wrong. Shortly after Creech left for Nicaragua, Virginia Reynolds and Clarence Nodstrom went to have a talk with District Superintendent Joseph Bethea.

The governing of Methodist churches is an odd mix of hierarchical and grass-roots approaches. The day-to-day running of the local church is handled by committees formed from the congregation. These committees manage the church's finances, including such matters as setting the minister's salary. But it is the district superintendent, acting in the name of the bishop, who actually appoints ministers to churches and, if the need arises, removes them.

In their meeting with the district superintendent, Virginia Reynolds told him bluntly that Jimmy Creech had to go. She said that "everyone in the church felt" that Jimmy's ministry to homosexuals was an affront to God and was ruining the reputation of Fairmont. She repeated this message on several follow-up visits.

Meanwhile, the Wesley Bible Class had asked Margie, the church secretary, for a set of mailing labels to the entire congregation. Margie wasn't quite sure what to do about this. Obviously, something was up, and whatever it was, it hadn't been cleared through the PPRC. Eventually District Superintendent Bethea suggested that she just go ahead and give them the labels and see what happened.

What happened was that the Wesley class sent out copies of its resolution condemning anyone who "embraces homosexuality, or those who practice it," along with a copy of Creech's original letter to area clergy about the Gay and Lesbian Pride Parade. Shortly thereafter, they began circulating a petition through the congregation:

> We the undersigned members of Fairmont United Methodist Church, Raleigh, NC, who are in good standing, state that we can no longer have as our pastor Reverend James Creech, for reasons presented to you in some letters and statements from one of our members, Mrs. Virginia Reynolds, who has met and talked with you several times. Mrs. Reynolds represents our feelings on these subjects.
>
> We believe this to be a conference matter and, therefore, it is respectfully requested that the Conference make a change, immediately, and transfer the Reverend Mr. Creech and replace him with a pastor who will follow the rules of the *Discipline* as it applies to the local church; a person who will minister to the congregation, preach and teach the Gospel according to the Holy Bible and the *Discipline* of the United Methodist Church.[7]

When Jimmy returned in early August, he learned that the petition had been presented to the bishop with the signatures of eighty older members of his congregation.

On August 11, the Pastor-Parish Relations Committee met with the district superintendent to discuss the situation. Most of them believed that the superintendent would probably solve the problem by moving Jimmy to another church. Historically, the Methodist denomination has dealt with conflict by avoidance. In the short run, it makes for harmonious churches, but in the long run it means that no divisive topic ever gets confronted or resolved.

"It's so seldom that I've ever seen any controversial issue brought out and talked about," comments the Reverend Bill Sharpe. "I've seen lots of 'em swept under the carpet. And I've seen lots of pastors moved because they got into controversy that might have split the church."

On this occasion, however, Superintendent Bethea informed the Committee that he had already consulted with Bishop Minnick on this matter. The bishop had determined that Reverend Creech's ministry was not in violation of either Scripture or the Methodist *Discipline*. Given that, the superintendent saw no reason to move Reverend Creech at this time. Fairmont would have to deal with its own problems.

In addition to being on the Pastor-Parish Relations Committee, Walter Brock was also the chair of the Administrative Committee, which made him the highest-ranking lay member within Fairmont. As a lawyer, Brock felt sure that if he could persuade everyone to sit down and talk reasonably, they could somehow work the whole thing out. Let people express their concerns; get them talking about the issue rather than firing off resolutions at each other. He suggested that the PPRC schedule an open meeting for the next Sunday night.

The committee decided not to invite Reverend Creech, feeling that his presence might inhibit people from speaking their minds. They wanted members of the congregation to talk about their feelings, whether they were pleasant or not. One of the committee's documents notes: "It was recognized that the meeting could be divisive, or could be the beginning of a mending process."[8]

Inhibition did not turn out to be a problem. That Sunday evening the church was full as it had never been before. The balcony was full, the downstairs pews were full, and there were people standing in the aisles. Passions ran high, and people expressed their opinions bluntly.

Older members accused Creech of perverting the word of God, of destroying the reputation of Fairmont, and of recruiting homosexuals to join the church. Some of them asserted that Creech must be a closet homosexual himself. Others said that his teenage son, Patrick, must be gay, or Creech wouldn't be so interested in the subject. They talked about how they had built this church, had nurtured it, and now wanted it to be a safe, comfortable place in which to spend their later years. They did not want some crazy social activist filling up their pews with deviants.

The younger members were shocked by such a display of open hatred. Although many of them didn't approve of homosexuality, almost none of them were as absolutely outraged by it as the older members were. As young adults, they'd all seen gay and lesbian issues discussed on the news, and they had even gotten used to seeing a few gay and lesbian characters on their network sitcoms. Even if they didn't agree with homosexuality, they couldn't find it as shocking as the older members did. They were already used to seeing gays as humans. Maybe flawed humans, but certainly not monsters.

Only a few of the younger members were willing to stand up and publicly embrace Reverend Creech's ministry to the gays. But many of them were willing to stand up for Jimmy's right to say what he thought and to do what he believed was right. If Jimmy felt that he was called by God to help these people, then they were willing to let him follow that call. They could respect his right to have an opinion, even if they didn't all agree with it.

The people who were most deeply moved by the meeting, though, were the college students from the Methodist campus ministry. Bill Sharpe still remembers that night well.

"If you know anything about college students today, they're fairly conservative. But on that night they saw people they looked up to as older people, mentors, grandmothers, and grandfathers. They saw these gentle people just come unraveled because they were so upset by someone stirring the traditions of the church and challenging the traditions of the church. They saw hatred coming out of these people, and fire, and venom. And they saw things in people that they had not seen before.

"A lot of the reaction from the college students was very sad. Some of them stood at the microphone and just cried, trying to say 'I don't understand. Why would the church not allow this person to say and believe what he feels and thinks?'

"And that would come even from people who were vehemently against

homosexuality, who quoted the Bible in defense of being antihomosexual. They just couldn't understand how the church could respond in that way to a person trying to respond to God's call."

In retrospect, Walter Brock recalls that night as the start of the real split in the congregation. "The lawyer in me said, 'Well, let's just all sit down and talk about it.' Which is one of the lessons I've learned—that sometimes, it doesn't do any good to talk about it."

Immediately after the open meeting, the Pastor-Parish Relations Committee met to decide what to do about Jimmy Creech. It was still possible to get rid of him, if they were determined to do it. His yearly evaluation was due with the bishop. If the PPRC recommended that Reverend Creech be moved, the bishop would probably bow to the wishes of the committee. Before they could even discuss the matter, however, two conservative members of the PPRC resigned in protest.

Brock was flabbergasted by the maneuver. Here was their chance to voice an opinion, to give their advice, and to cast their vote. Instead, they were walking away. Weren't they all supposed to be working together, to try and keep the church from coming apart? After some debate, and much grumbling about the two departed members, the PPRC voted unanimously to request that Jimmy Creech continue to serve as Fairmont's pastor.

After that decision was announced, the split in the congregation grew rapidly. Some of the older members resigned from Fairmont and went across town to Highland Methodist. A few, who blamed Bishop Minnick for not firing Creech earlier, left the denomination altogether. Those who did stay made a point of skipping the worship service and going directly to the men's and women's Bible classes. They also found a multitude of other ways to make their displeasure apparent. "Some of us on the Staff-Parish Relations Committee didn't become very popular folks," recalls Brock. "To this day there are still people in the church who won't look me in the eye, who won't shake my hand, who walk the other way anytime they get the chance."

The hostility that the PPRC experienced was nothing compared with what was vented on Creech himself. His face was ripped out of youth group photos on the bulletin board. Someone started going through his trash and reading his discarded correspondence. Notes got slipped under his door: "Calling all queers! Calling all gays! There will be a meeting at

Creech Homosexual Church (formerly Fairmont United Methodist Church) at 7:30 on September 15, 1988. All weirdoes invited." One Sunday morning, as Creech was greeting people after worship, a man looked at him coldly and said, "I think what you're doing here is the work of the Devil. I think the bishop has sent you here to run all the old folks off and make this a church for young people and homosexuals."[9]

Rumors ran wild through the church, revealing various people's fears about what Creech was really up to. Some said that he was recruiting homosexuals to join the church. Others said that he was going to turn Fairmont into a gay church. A couple even said that he was encouraging children to become homosexuals. And one woman was earnestly telling people that Creech had been unlocking the sanctuary during the week so that gay men could have sex in it.

Sometimes, the rumors and harassment had unexpected side effects. Steven Churchill was one of the college students who had begun attending Fairmont through the campus ministry. He remembers watching for weeks as the attacks on Jimmy grew more and more hateful. The more outrageous the attacks got, the more convinced Steven became that there was something deeply wrong with the people making them. Steven had always believed what he'd been told growing up—that homosexuality was an abomination, a thing to be ashamed of. But watching all of the hatred directed at Jimmy, Steven began to question if Creech was really the one who had the problem.

Unlike Jimmy, Steven had not had the courage to march in the Pride Parade that summer. But that fall he went to his pastor and thanked Reverend Creech for standing up for him. For the first time, Steven told someone in his church that he was gay. Later, it was in his pastor's offices and with his pastor's help that he broke the news to his parents.

Another person who was influenced by the attacks on Creech was his superior, Bishop Minnick. After seeing firsthand how much hatred could be unleashed by the mere discussion of homosexuality, Bishop Minnick decided that it was a problem that needed to be tackled decisively. He wrote a letter to all the Methodist clergy under his authority, encouraging them to attend RRNGLE's second conference, the topic of which was going to be "Homophobia in the Religious Community."

"This letter is my endorsement of this event and my encouragement to you to avail yourselves of this opportunity to enhance your understanding of the fears, the hate and the hostility toward homosexual persons and their families. These emotions are expressed in so many painful and destructive ways in our churches and society. Homophobia is an urgent pastoral care issue which we need to address."[10]

The rumors and attacks on Creech that fall seem to have been more spontaneous acts of rage than any coherent plot to drive him out. But at the end of 1988, the anti-Creech faction finally found the tool that would give them enough leverage to dispose of the Reverend—money. Although the older members were no longer a majority of the congregation, they were heavy contributors. In 1989 they began a concerted effort to break the church financially.

Although no formal ultimatum was issued, the faction made it clear that the offerings would not start flowing again until Creech was removed. Since the older members still cared for the church, they could often be approached for a donation for a specific purpose—a new paint job for the building or a piece of furniture for the office. But they always made sure that not one penny went to Fairmont's general operating budget, out of which both the minister's salary was paid and donations to the North Carolina Methodist Conference were made. As the anti-Creech faction saw it, since they didn't want him here, they weren't going to pay his salary. And until the conference moved him, they weren't going to support it, either.

Fairmont's financial situation deteriorated rapidly. Although new members had been attracted by Creech's work on social justice issues, they were not nearly enough to make up for the lost income from the older members. The church was only taking in two-thirds of what it needed to operate, and the budget had to be cut to the bone. Fairmont made no contribution to the North Carolina Methodist Conference that year. Sunday school teachers couldn't afford to buy lesson materials for the children. Sometimes there wasn't even money to buy paper or pencils for the office.

By spring, Jimmy was beginning to show signs of wear. The church could only hold out for so long like this, and the constant infighting was starting to get to him. Even Brock, who strongly supported him, suggested that he might want to resign.

"I suggested to Jimmy that he just ask the bishop to move him, because of the personal drain it was on him. It was bad, day to day. Small, ugly things. The isolation, the innuendo, the backbiting. It was horrible. It had to be hard to get up and come in. You had to be a tough person."

In March, Jimmy went to the other ministers in RRNGLE to tell them that he was thinking of throwing in the towel. The situation seemed insurmountable. But the response from the other ministers surprised him. As they saw it, what was going on at Fairmont was not simply an internal issue of church politics. If Jimmy were forced to knuckle under, it would be a long, long time before any other minister in Raleigh would risk taking a stand in support of gay rights. RRNGLE members believed that this was an issue for the whole Raleigh religious community, and the whole community needed to solve it. They told Creech to hang tight, and they'd see what they could do.

Over the next few months, Fairmont received donations from a number of surprising sources, including several Roman Catholic priests and a rabbi. A couple of local churches in other denominations took up collections on behalf of Fairmont. The money only totaled four thousand dollars, but it provided a much needed boost in morale to both Jimmy and his congregation.

The rest of the year was still a rough one, but as is often the case with difficult times, many people now look back on 1989 with a certain fondness. There was a sense of shared sacrifice, of pulling together for a purpose. Jimmy decided to stick it out, and the Pastor-Parish Relations Committee backed him up, once again asking the bishop to let Jimmy remain as pastor. Because the church was only taking in two-thirds of its minimum budget, Jimmy volunteered to cut his own pay to two-thirds of what it had been the year before.

"The cream always rises to the top in a crisis," says Brock of the people who held the church together during that year. "The biggest thing they did was that they stayed. And they continued to be your friends. They continued to love your children. They didn't allow this thing to divide people who had a bond to begin with. It almost got to be the pro-Jimmy and the anti-Jimmy groups. But they didn't allow their feelings about being against his leadership in the church to divide us."

In his annual advisory to the bishop, Creech summed up the situation at Fairmont and his reasons for wanting to stay in spite of all the controversy.

"The reaction has come from a leadership core that has guided Fairmont Church for most of its first fifty years. This leadership has been strong, good and effective. But, it has been reluctant to be open to new leadership and new directions. In many ways, while my involvement with gay/lesbian rights was the catalyst for the reaction, the fundamental issue has been the transition to a newer, broader, more fluid leadership. The recognition that many of the former leaders have died, that there is less control, and that there are new ideas and visions of ministry held by others who are challenging for leadership, have made the older leadership fearful that they will 'lose their church.' While the older leadership has reacted against my ministry, the new leadership has been supportive and encouraging. Should I be moved now, it will be a sign to the newer leadership that growth in vision and ministry is not possible at Fairmont."

Equally important, though, was the message that Creech felt his transfer would send to other Methodist ministers in the state.

"Should I be moved because of the controversy regarding gay/lesbian rights, it will be a signal to the clergy that the Conference will not support prophetic risk-taking on behalf of peace and justice. It would indicate that the true priorities are tranquility and the status quo."[11]

One way or another, Fairmont managed to make it through that summer and fall. But by the end of 1989 it was clear that it was taking all the church's energy just to stay afloat. Fairmont faced a choice: it could either support Reverend Creech's stand, or it could do all the other things a church wants to do—support charities, work on other social causes—it could not do both. Jimmy knew that Fairmont could only hold out for so long. He also knew that it was only a matter of time before the story broke in the press. He'd been putting off reporters from two local papers for several months now. His time was running out anyway, and if the story was going to run, he wanted to have some say about what went into it.

"When someone asks you for help, you don't ask permission to respond," Jimmy said to Melinda Ruley, a reporter from the *Independent Weekly*. "People never really choose the causes or the time to take a stand. Our responsibility is to be responsive. I look back and almost feel that it's been out of my hands.

"What the members of Fairmont need to realize is this: I didn't bring the issue of homophobia with me—and it won't leave with me."[12]

The article ran in January of 1990, under the headline "Ministering to Our Fears." Although Ruley faithfully tried to get both sides of the story, she found that none of the anti-Creech faction was willing to talk to her. Even though she had a list of eighty people who had signed the petition to have Creech removed, no one she contacted was willing to be interviewed or talk about his or her feelings publicly.[13]

As Jimmy says, "Telling the truth can get you in a lot of trouble." After the *Independent* article ran, the story broke wide open. The other local papers jumped on the story, and television crews began turning up at the church to question members as they left services. Other Methodist ministers issued stinging condemnations of both Jimmy and Fairmont, attacks that were edited down to soundbites for the evening news.

At this point many of the members who had been sitting on the fence joined the anti-Creech camp. "They felt embarrassed, they felt that the church had been given a bad name," says Creech. It was one thing to debate the matter internally; it was quite another to have the whole world know that they were talking about it. That March, the Pastor-Parish Relations Committee asked the bishop to reassign Reverend Creech to a different church. Jimmy conceded, and told the bishop he would be willing to move.

With Creech gone, there was a shift in the congregation, as some people came back and other people left. Steven Churchill quit the church in disgust, leaving not only Fairmont but the entire Methodist denomination. Walter Brock, in contrast, decided to stay at Fairmont and try to make a go of it. He admits that there are still some hard feelings between those who left the church during its difficult year and those who stayed. Although the two groups can make polite conversation, there are certain things that they cannot talk about with each other.

For Jimmy, life got even more difficult for a while. Theoretically, Methodist ministers are guaranteed employment for life once they're ordained. They go where the church tells them, and the church makes sure that they always have someplace to go.

In North Carolina, the process of appointing ministers to Methodist churches runs from April through May. Throughout the spring, though, Creech was told that the bishop was having trouble finding a suitable church because of all the publicity surrounding him. The bishop did not want a repeat of what had happened at Fairmont. By the time of the North Carolina Conference in early June, the only churches left were two rural churches in Vance County, and Jimmy was offered these as an appointment. After the conference, however, both churches wrote the bishop to say that they would not accept Creech as their pastor, and if the bishop insisted on sending him anyway, they would not support his ministry in any way whatsoever, including attending his sermons or paying his salary. Bishop Minnick bowed to their wishes, and Creech was without a parish.

This meant that Creech, being a Methodist minister, suddenly had neither a job nor a roof over his head. The new minister for Fairmont was moving into the parsonage, and Jimmy had nowhere to go. At the last minute, a friend offered him the spare bedroom in her house, so Jimmy and his son lived there for several weeks.

During those weeks, Jimmy spent a lot of time thinking about his future, about what he wanted to do with his life and how he could still serve the Church. Finally, he requested a meeting with the bishop and his cabinet to suggest "that they allow me to start a new congregation in the Triangle. In the work I had been doing on peace and justice issues, I had discovered that there was a large number of people who had been disaffected by the institutional church. They were very spiritual people, very religious people, but they were just offended by the institutional church. I wanted to start a congregation, pulling in people who were interested in being part of a church and also being a part of working for justice together. And it would be a church that would never have a building, that we would be intentional in sharing space with schools or whatever. But our primary focus would be to work on social justice issues.

"And they said, 'That's a good idea. But you're not the person to do it, because it would become a gay church. And we don't want a gay United Methodist church.'

"Then they offered me three little churches south of Wilmington that they had not appointed a minister to because they were dying, and they were just waiting for them to die out. And I declined. So I was without work. Without anything."

In 1987, Jimmy Creech had come to Raleigh with a reputation as a rising star in the methodist conference. By 1990 it was clear that his career as a Methodist minister was over.

For six months after that meeting with the bishop, Creech survived through the kindness of friends. The Community United Church of Christ donated money so that he would have something to live off of, and a friend who managed a rental property let Jimmy and his son stay in a vacant apartment. Finally, Jimmy landed a job with the North Carolina Council of Churches, an ecumenical group of which the Methodist church is a member.

Creech now holds the position of Program Associate. It's a job that focuses on social justice issues, and one that he enjoys. He works on criminal justice, health care justice, and trying to improve the lives of North Carolina's migrant farm workers. It's not the same as having a congregation, but it is work that he believes in.

"I guess that not really much was achieved by all that happened, in terms of real change," he says. Then he thinks for a moment. "Except, maybe, just the public awareness that was created. When Pullen and Binkley considered their respective issues, some of the ice had been broken.

"So maybe there was a little something positive that came out of it."

CHAPTER 2

Fellowship of Believers:
Pullen Baptist

It's hard to decide just what to think of Willie Pilkington. People have described him as a martyr, a criminal, a civil rights leader, and an annoying media hound. The facts, as well as I can determine, are these:

In 1978 Pilkington was arrested in Raleigh and charged with soliciting sex from a minor. His twelve-year-old accuser told police that Pilkington had offered him money for sex, and gave them Willie's description and license plate number. There were no other witnesses or collaborating evidence, so the case boiled down to Pilkington's word against the boy's. In court, DA Linda Mobley effectively discredited Pilkington by asking him, under oath, if he had ever been convicted of drunken or reckless driving. Pilkington answered that he had not. Mobley then showed the jury the criminal record of one William Pilkington, who had been convicted of both charges. The jury concluded that Pilkington was a liar and found him guilty. Willie, however, had been telling the truth. The record belonged to a different man of the same name.

Facing four years in prison and with no money for a lawyer to file an appeal, Willie Pilkington turned to the gay community. Word circulated, and eventually a group of seven prominent gay men met to consider the problem. The men were interested in mounting a challenge to North Carolina's "Crimes against Nature" law, which prohibits intercourse between consenting adults of the same sex. Willie's case did not quite meet their needs. For one thing, soliciting sex from a minor is an altogether different act than sex between consenting adults. The seven did *not* support the right of adults to have sex with children. After working so hard to dispel the myth that gay men were habitual child molesters, the group was uncomfortable getting involved with just such an accusation. And there were nagging doubts about Willie's innocence. On the one hand, both Willie and his accuser claimed never to have met before the incident. Why would the boy make up such as story? But in fact the testimony of children is notoriously unreliable, which has led to more than one erroneous witch hunt.

The one thing that was clear was that Pilkington had not received a fair trial. The seven men formed the North Carolina Human Rights Campaign Fund, which is still in existence. Willie quickly showed he was willing to work hard on his own behalf, traveling the state, speaking as an openly gay man, and raising funds for the new organization and his own defense.

Pilkington's appeals were consistently rejected by the North Carolina state courts, which ruled that although the DA had introduced false evidence, she had done so unknowingly and "in good faith." Finally, a federal court ordered a new trial in 1982, at which time the state accepted Pilkington's four months' time served in prison in exchange for a plea of "no contest."

By the 1980s Pilkington's interest in gay rights had grown beyond his own case. He became an important activist in North Carolina, starting two gay organizations (one of which is still operating), hounding the local press for better coverage of gay and lesbian issues, and working in the election campaigns of several city council members. In 1987 when Nancy Kepple was trying to rally support for expanding Raleigh's nondiscrimination clause, Willie was one of the people she approached. He did what he could—rounding up speakers, calling the local papers with information, and appearing as a guest on a couple of local radio call-in shows.

"It's not that I don't want to help," said the Reverend Mahan Siler, "it's just that I have no idea what I would say."

Nancy Kepple had just asked him to testify at a public hearing on the need for civil rights protection for homosexuals—not the sort of thing that Southern Baptist ministers get called on to do very often. Still, Nancy had known Mahan back when he'd been the director of a school of pastoral care over in Winston-Salem, and she thought she could appeal to his sense of fair play. When Mahan asked, "Well, what do I know about homosexuality?" Nancy offered to give him an education. "I'll introduce you to Willie Pilkington," she said. "He's a gay man and he can tell you all about the harassment that he's faced because of it."

"Of course," she added, "we'll have to drive out to see him at his house. He hasn't been getting around so well since he was shot."

Sadly, Pilkington seems to be one of those people with the passion and drive to get projects off the ground, but not the interpersonal skills to build and sustain them. Throughout the 1980s, his conflicts with people who should have been his allies grew steadily worse. Three weeks before the hearings, a meeting with other activists ended just short of a shouting match.

He decided to get out of town and cool off for a while. He drove to Fayetteville, where he'd been stationed in the army, and went to a straight bar where he figured no one would be talking gay politics. He met a man there who, Pilkington says, invited him home to meet his wife. Instead, the man drove Willie out to the edge of a cornfield near Clinton, North Carolina, and pulled a gun on him. When Willie tried to run away, the man shot him in the back.

To his attacker's surprise, Willie kept running and made it into the cover of the cornfield. The bullet had glanced off a rib, passing through his body but missing all of his internal organs. Though bleeding, Willie managed to find his way across the cornfield to a trailer home, where the occupants called an ambulance for him.

What surprised Mahan was not the story of Willie's shooting, but the sheriff's department's reaction to it. Because Willie was conscious when he arrived at the hospital, he tried to tell the sheriff everything he could about the man who had shot him. But Willie noticed that the sheriff didn't seem to be taking any of that down. Instead, he kept asking Willie where he worked, what he was doing in the area, and how they could get in touch with him. There was something odd about the way the doctors were behaving, too.

What Willie didn't know was that the sheriff had already told the attending physician that Willie was a suspect in a criminal investigation, and that he was a "queer." He also told the doctor that Willie had been shot as he attacked someone, so the bullet had entered from the front. The doctor entered this information into Willie's medical records, in spite of its obvious inconsistency with the wound. A bullet, as it enters a body, makes a small, round hole. As it leaves, it makes a large, irregular tear. Even a cursory examination showed that Willie had been shot from behind.

Shortly after Willie was attacked, a man pulled into a nearby convenience store and asked the cashier if he had seen a man come running through the parking lot. The cashier had not. The man told him to watch out for someone, because he had just shot a queer, and the queer might still be walking. The unknown man then drove off in a hurry. Somewhat alarmed, the convenience store clerk phoned the sheriff to report the man's comment, along with his license plate number.

The sheriff's department quickly got in contact with Willie's assailant, who admitted the shooting. He claimed that Willie had made a sexual advance toward him, and that he had simply defended himself. The sheriff's department decided that the man was not a threat to society and that there was no need to take him into custody or even to relieve him of his firearm. Instead, they launched an investigation of Willie for violating North Carolina's "Crimes against Nature" law and alerted the State Bureau of Investigation (SBI).

By the time that Willie told his story to Mahan Siler, the SBI had given up on its investigation. For one thing, Willie had discovered the mistake in his medical records. Upon being forced to examine the wound, the attending physician had recanted his statement and changed the records to show that Willie had been shot in the back. Even the SBI had to admit that it is difficult to get shot in the back while attacking someone.

Furthermore, the SBI had realized that Pilkington wasn't likely to roll over quietly. Willie had insisted that witnesses be present during his questioning. When summoned for an interrogation, he had brought along Nancy Kepple and an Episcopal priest, Jim Lewis. Usually, those accused of violating the "Crimes against Nature" law are too embarrassed to put up much of a court fight. This was not true of Willie. The SBI would have to make its case before a judge and jury. In the absence of any evidence, it backed out.

The sheriff's department also dropped its investigation of Willie after Reverend Lewis had a few words with the investigating officer. Dressed in his clerical collar and speaking very calmly, Lewis talked about the sheriff's department's responsibility to protect all victims, including gay ones. "When he started using words like that," says Willie, "the guy started listening. But then a minister was talking, so he was really listening to a minister is what it amounted to. And he was hearing words that he had never heard a minister say before."

After hearing Willie's story and Nancy Kepple's description of the SBI's behavior, Reverend Siler agreed to testify at the public hearing.

Mahan Siler still remembers the hearing well. "Being placed on the docket toward the end of the evening, I had to sit through the other testimonies. Again and again I heard homosexuals go public with their experiences of discrimination. Particularly alarming were the illustrations of frequent condemnation by the Church. Hearing so many back-to-back examples brought me to a decision—to go public with a different kind of message from the Church, one more congruent, I believe, with our mission."

Mahan became one of the founding members of the Raleigh Religious Network for Gay and Lesbian Equality. The next spring, his church, Pullen Baptist, served as the site for RRNGLE's first conference. And in July of 1988, Mahan walked beside Jimmy Creech in the North Carolina Gay and Lesbian Pride Parade.

Like Creech, Siler paid a price for his participation in that parade. When Southeastern Baptist Seminary heard about it, both Mahan and his wife were fired from their jobs as instructors. Still, Mahan's situation at Pullen Baptist was quite different from Jimmy's at Fairmont Methodist. Siler had been at Pullen for a long time. He had prayed with the members, married them, baptized them, and buried their loved ones. However they might feel about the parade, it was, after all, only one event in a long relationship.

There was also the nature of Pullen itself. Southern Baptists tend to be very conservative—most of their congregations are all white, many believe that women should be subordinate to their husbands, and homosexuality is a topic that isn't even mentioned in polite company. However, Southern Baptist churches are also given a great deal of freedom to set their own policies and explore their own beliefs. This freedom allowed Pullen to march to a different drummer. It was one of those rare churches that has a tradition of facing up to controversy. Pullen had been a strong advocate of integration as far back as the 1950s, a time when many Southern states still had laws banning interracial marriages, and when most Southern Baptist churches were preaching that God intended the races to be separate. During the 1960s, Pullen had taken an early stand against the Vietnam War. The church had long had a reputation for being out on the edge of social change, for dealing with issues while other churches were still hoping they would go away. This strength was, in fact, one of the things that drew people into Pullen—a belief that unlike most churches, which seemed to look inward, this church looked outward and tried to work for justice in the world.

None of which is to say that the members of Pullen's congregation were ready to endorse homosexuality at the end of the 1980s. They were, however, ready to start talking about it.

It was in Jimmy Creech's office at Fairmont that Steven Churchill had first told his parents he was gay. His mother cried for three days after that, and spent hours reading him the scriptural prohibitions on homosexuality from the letters of Paul. His father said nothing. His brothers had the most direct solution to the problem: they wanted to hire a prostitute to "straighten him out."

Eventually, though, the Churchill family managed to make peace with one another. Steven found himself wondering why the congregation at Fairmont couldn't do the same. All that Reverend Creech was saying was that people like Steven were as deserving of grace as anyone else. Seeing what the older members put Jimmy through slowly soured Steven on both Fairmont and the Methodist denomination. It also convinced him of the need to stand up for himself. The world was not a just place, and something needed to be done about it.

Steven began putting some of his energies into campus politics, and by February of 1989, he was serving as co-chair of the Gay and Lesbian Student Union at North Carolina State. The group was hosting a social for gay and lesbian students, and one of the people to turn up was Kevin Turner, looking very uncomfortable. Kevin had just begun to work on his Ph.D. in physics, and this was the first gay party he'd ever been to. Steven went over to talk to him and try to make him feel a little less nervous. To his surprise, the two of them hit it off, and a week later they went out on their first date.

Kevin was a Southern Baptist and a member of Pullen Baptist Church, just a couple of blocks from campus. As the two of them started dating more seriously, Steven began attending church with Kevin from time to time.

In 1990 Pat Long came before Pullen's Board of Deacons and began telling them about herself. Although she had been a member of the church for eleven years, none of the deacons knew, until then, that she was a lesbian. Pat talked about why she had hidden so much of her life from her spiritual community, and about how much hiding it had hurt her. She told the deacons of how she had had to grieve the death of her lover alone, without help from her church. A straight woman who is widowed has the whole congregation to lean on. A lesbian has only herself.

At the conclusion of her speech, Pat asked for Pullen to become a "reconciling" church—that is, a congregation that explicitly welcomes gay men and lesbians as full members. She suggested a year-long education program, during which people could read about homosexuality and discuss their feelings, followed by a vote of the congregation as a whole.

The deacons declined to initiate the vote—it was too likely to turn into a divisive event. But they did think that the education process sounded like a good idea. The diaconate set up a series of forums—small meetings where people could discuss the causes of homosexuality, the biblical issues around it, the civil rights implications, and their own personal feelings.

All in all, the forums were judged to be a success. People who attended them felt that they left with a better understanding. Pat worried, though, that most of the congregation had not participated in them.

On November 3, 1991, two and a half years after Kevin and Steve's first date, Reverend Siler presented an unusual request to Pullen's Board of Deacons. He asked them to think about it carefully, and to reflect on it for a full month before taking any action. His request came in the form of a written statement.

On September 12, 1991, Kevin Turner and Steven Churchill came to my office inviting me to officiate at the blessing of their same gender union (called the Blessing of the Holy Union). . . . They have requested that the service be held at Pullen.

I have counseled with them for three sessions and am satisfied that the motivation for their request as well as their commitment to God, the Church, and each other warrant a positive response. In spite of the complexity and controversial nature of their request, I feel led by my best judgment to serve as pastor at such a ceremony of blessing and commitment.

You give me the freedom to make my own decisions about assuming the responsibility of officiating at the blessing of heterosexual couples. But this request is different. As far as I'm aware, no Pullen pastor has ever performed such a ceremony.

I do not function independently. I, as your pastor, represent Christ's ministry and the Pullen congregation as well as my own conscience. I stand accountable to all three. As elected leaders of Pullen, I need you to share with me the responsibility of seeking the mind of Christ on this matter.[1]

Siler went on to outline his thinking on the scriptural objections that could be raised against performing a homosexual union, concluding: "The Bible, in [its] few references to homosexual acts, condemns them as expressions of lust, homosexual rape, pagan idolatry, cult prostitution, and pederasty. In other words, exploitive, promiscuous sexual acts—whether heterosexual or homosexual—are condemned as sinful and destructive."

Siler did not believe that any of these prohibitions applied to a caring, committed relationship between two men. Moreover, he saw many reasons for wanting to encourage stable relationships like the one between Kevin and Steve.

Promiscuity is rampant among both homosexuals and heterosexuals. Here is the place for us to stand—the support of such committed relationships. Our society gives little encouragement to homosexuals who desire a monogamous, loving relationship. . . . I have come to believe that the church, of all institutions, should encourage the blessing and nurturance of such covenants.

I wanted you to understand my position. But equally I want you to understand my respect for the wisdom of Pullen. This extension of our ministry might be costly. . . . Therefore pledge with me the strong effort to provide each other a safe place, an open environment where fears, questions, disagreements, insights can be cherished. You deserved my clearest thinking about a response to this request from another Pullen member. Now, I ask you also to struggle with your sense of what should be our stance as a congregation. Only together, in a community that honors truth seeking and respects individual expressions of faith, can we most likely discern God's will.[2]

After reading Mahan's statement, a few of the deacons immediately said that the ceremony sounded like a great idea, a way of promoting traditional Christian values in the gay community. Others thought the whole idea was only one step short of devil worship.

Most of the deacons, though, wished that the whole "issue of homosexuality would just go away without requiring a decision from us."[3] This was the kind of issue that divided congregations and got people angry. No matter how they resolved the matter, someone was likely to get upset and leave the church over it—either gay members who felt unwelcome or conservative members who felt that the church was committing blasphemy. On the whole, everything would be a lot more peaceful if the question had never come up.

The deacons honored Reverend Siler's wishes, nevertheless, and agreed to spend a month thinking about it. Pat Long, who by this time had been elected a deacon, suddenly found herself serving as the gay resource for the group. As the only open homosexual that most of the deacons knew, she found herself answering questions that ranged from the astoundingly naive to the embarrassingly personal. Still, it was good to know that the other deacons were trying to understand.

The Baptist faith is based on what is known as the "priesthood of the believer." This tenet states that anyone can learn the will of God for himself or herself. You don't need to be told what to believe by a priest; you need only look to the Bible and to your own heart and sincerely ask God to help you find the truth.

As a result of this belief, the Baptist church is run in a very democratic, grass-roots fashion. Decisions, rather than being handed down from a bishop or a cardinal, are made by a vote of the individual believers in the congregation. This, in fact, is another important article of the Baptist faith—the autonomy of the local church. Every Baptist congregation has the right to make the decisions that affect the life of its church. No higher authority can tell the members what to believe, whom to hire, or how to manage their finances.

When the diaconate met again in December, it was deeply divided. Fourteen of the deacons supported the union as a "positive expression of the church's ministry."[4] Four others were strongly opposed to the ceremony as incompatible with Scripture and likely to draw condemnation from other Southern Baptists. One deacon simply abstained from the whole matter. However, all nineteen of them supported Reverend Siler in his statement of conscience, and all were united on the correct course of action for a Baptist church. They unanimously agreed to put the matter to a vote of the congregation.

After the Christmas holidays, the diaconate sent a letter to every member of Pullen, informing them of the situation and asking them to attend a church meeting on February 9 to vote on the issue. The mailing also included the schedule for a series of meetings that would be held to discuss the matter, to share points of view, and to help people work through their feelings.

Over the next six weeks, fifteen small group meetings were held at the church and in the homes of members. They discussed the meaning of various scriptural passages and debated whether homosexuality was something innate that people are born with or something that they choose to become. One woman talked about her first husband, who had committed suicide because of the shame he felt for being gay. Several parents admitted that they had gay children, and spoke of their struggles to understand them. At nearly every meeting, some member of the church came out of the closet, announcing his or her homosexuality. These members spoke for the first time about the fear that had caused them to hide so long from their friends. For many other members of Pullen, this was the first time they realized that they knew a homosexual.

After the letter went out, it wasn't long before the press discovered the controversy. In early January Steven was called by a reporter for the *Raleigh*

News and Observer. At the end of the interview, the reporter asked if he could use Steven's full name in the story. The question caused Steven some hesitation—he wasn't out of the closet at work, and he didn't know how his boss would react. But he decided that withholding his name would make it look like he was ashamed of what they were doing. He told the reporter to go ahead and use his full name.

At work the next day, Steven nervously waited for someone to say something about the story. And waited. And waited. Finally he went to his boss, Patty, and asked what she'd thought of the article. She hadn't even noticed it. They got out the morning edition, and Steven showed her where it was. Patty took the paper to her supervisor, Kyle, and a few minutes later Steven was called into the office. Kyle succinctly informed Steven that he was a valued employee, that the company would tolerate no harassment of him, and that this made no difference in its assessment of him. That was all that he ever said on the matter. But apparently Kyle meant what he said: later that summer, he gave Steven a promotion.

Steven's family had a rougher time. Friends at his parents' Methodist church bluntly told them to rein in their son and put a stop to this foolishness. At work, his mother faced two days of complete silence from her co-workers. When she spoke to them, they turned away from her.

Along with the news articles came the protesters. Every Sunday during worship services, five or six people would picket Pullen. They would heckle members going in and out of the sanctuary, shouting at them and waving signs that said "God created Adam and Eve, not Adam and Steve!" and "This church is polluted. God is not here."

Although some of the youth from Pullen went out to invite the protesters in to worship, their invitations were always declined. They debated theology a bit, but neither side could do much to convince the other. Still, their conversations did turn up one interesting fact: the protesters were paid professionals, hired by a fundamentalist religious organization. (While some of the fundamentalists no doubt wanted to join the protest, they had their own Sunday morning services to attend.) On weekdays, they were being deployed on college campuses, to protest whatever their employer deemed to be the latest liberal threat to decency.

On February 2, the congregation gathered for a town meeting, to see if any sort of consensus was building. A couple of members spoke out vehemently against any sort of blessing of homosexuality, but it was clear that many of the conservative members had been rethinking their position. "This year has really made me aware that there is pain and hurt out there," said Mike Watts, a member of Pullen's Poteat Sunday school class. Poteat was the class that many of the older members of the congregation attended, and it contained some of those most violently opposed to the union.

"I didn't know any homosexual members by face or name until this year," Mike added. That was before he went to one of the small group meetings.

"I was much more adamantly opposed to the holy union before that meeting. I thought, 'Maybe if I knew who some of these people were, maybe if I could put a human face on it, I would feel differently, but right now I'm totally opposed to it.' And while I didn't change my vote, I did change my sensitivity.

"I was amazed. There were at least two, maybe three people that admitted they were homosexual. And I could see that these people were dear friends, they were Christians of many years whom I respected, who had made major contributions to the church in their own lives, in just devoting their lives to various things to help people. And yet they can be gay? That really made me look at things in a different light.

"It wasn't the scriptural arguments, or the arguments from medicine, or biology, or anything like that. It was seeing people that I really cared about, that I really respect. People who were intelligent human beings who obviously would not have chosen this way of life if they'd had any say so in the choice."

Yet with a week still to go before the vote, it was clear that Pullen was going to have a fight on its hands. There were strong passions on both sides of the debate, and some of the conservative members were threatening to leave the church if the union ceremony was performed. The diaconate was getting worried that the conflict might split the church, and they asked Reverend Siler if the matter could get quietly tabled somehow.

Siler approached Kevin and Steve with the idea, trying to put the best possible light on it. At least they'd brought up the issue, he pointed out. The congregation had been forced to talk about it, to think about it. The silence had been broken.

Kevin and Steve, however, were horrified by the suggestion that they drop the matter now. After all the church had gone through, after all that they had gone through, it was unthinkable. They weren't doing this as some sort of gay rights publicity stunt, they explained to Mahan. They wanted to be married, to have their union recognized in the eyes of their friends, their families, and their God.

Reverend Siler carried the message back to the deacons. Given that the church had already gone this far, the diaconate agreed to see the matter through to the end.

As on every Sunday, there were protesters in front of Pullen on the morning of February 9. As no one had thought to pay them to come back for the meeting that evening, however, they didn't.

It was the most well-attended congregational meeting that Pullen had ever seen. Kevin stood downstairs, with the voting members of the congregation, while Steven waited up in the balcony with the observers. Looking out at the people below him, Steven saw face after face of people who he knew were going to vote in favor of the union. He was sure that the resolution would pass when the vote was taken that night.

But the first motion passed that evening was to *not* take the vote at that meeting. Instead, ballots would be mailed out to all registered members of the congregation, who would be given two weeks to return them. Kevin and other pro-union members protested this decision loudly. As they saw it, anyone who hadn't come down to the church for the vote had probably never bothered to come to any of the discussion groups, either. Switching to a mail vote would be turning the decision over to people who had never given them a chance to discuss the issue, to explain what they were asking for. But the argument from Pullen's conservative members was difficult to refute—if Pullen was going to take a controversial public stance like this, then every member of the church ought to be consulted.

The rest of the meeting was spent in hammering out the language of the four resolutions that would be included on the mail-in ballot. The first of these was so watered down that it was almost impossible for anyone to disagree with: "We invite as members of Pullen all who believe in God revealed in Christ and seek to worship and serve that God."

The second resolution was more substantive, asking if the congregation welcomed gays and lesbians into full membership. The third was the meat of the matter—would the congregation support the union and allow the church building to be used for the ceremony. The fourth was a recommendation that Pullen establish a task force to study how a holy union service should be conducted, and what "biblical and theological underpinnings" existed for it.

The church office mailed the ballots out over the next few days.

On February 27, five of the deacons got together to count the ballots. They tallied the votes and then had to sit on the totals for three difficult days, until the results could be properly announced after Sunday services.

On March 1, Reverend Siler broke the news. As expected, the first proposition passed by a whopping fifty-to-one margin. A slightly smaller fraction of the church, 94 percent, had voted to welcome gays and lesbians into full membership. Seventy-five percent had voted to establish the task force to study same-sex unions. And 64 percent had voted in favor of performing Kevin and Steve's union ceremony as an appropriate part of the church's mission. The wedding was on.

Outside Pullen, television camera crews were set up to record the members' reactions as they left worship. The story of the Southern Baptist church that would marry two men was front-page news Monday morning, and not only in Raleigh. Pullen's office was flooded with phone calls from across the country, some furious with it for condoning sin, others praising it for promoting justice and monogamy.

Not all of the calls were made in a Christian spirit. Later in the week, a postal inspector dropped by the church office to instruct the staff on the danger of letter bombs.

In the middle of all this controversy, Kevin and Steve were rushing to make plans for the wedding. Because Pullen's vote had been delayed by two weeks, the March 15 date they'd chosen was now only a couple of weeks away. Complicating the rush was the need for secrecy—if word got out about the exact date, the protesters might crash the ceremony and try to disrupt it.

Kevin and Steve had expected a few awkward moments in setting up a wedding for two men. But to their surprise, most of the people they dealt with simply took the situation in stride. When they went shopping for a cake, for example, the decorator asked, "Well, where's the bride?"

"There is no bride," said Kevin, expecting trouble.

Without even blinking, the decorator looked at Steven, said "Oh, that's fine," and went on with his sales pitch.

The question of wedding presents worked itself out in a similar fashion. Kevin and Steve knew that straight couples usually registered with a department store, to cut down on confusion. The trouble was, neither of them knew what would happen if they tried to register as two men. Finally, Steve bit the bullet and phoned up the local Belks, part of a fairly large Southern chain.

"Do you register gay couples?" he asked the woman who answered the phone.

"Oh yeah," she responded.

Not sure that she understood, Steven decided to clarify. "I mean, you know, two *men*."

"Yeah," said the saleswoman, "that's what I figured you meant." Sure enough, when the two of them went down to pick out their china pattern, all of the sales staff were very helpful and polite.

The fifteenth of March finally came, and with the exception of the security measures, it was a most traditional Southern wedding. Because the date of the union had been kept out of the papers, there were no protesters. Still, a security sweep was made before the ceremony, and a pair of greeters checked guests' names off against an approved list as they came in the door. About two hundred friends and family gathered for the event. Steven's parents, having reconciled to the idea, attended. Kevin's parents also came, as well as most of the people from his physics lab, and his sister sang. There were flowers, there was music, and there was more than one tear shed.

"You are letting Satan run your church," one woman said in her letter to Mahan Siler.

"When God says homos are an abomination, he means it," wrote a couple from Florida. "You are supposed to TEACH them right, rather than trying to please a majority."

"Sir, Every person who gave credence to the idea of 'blessing homosexual unions' and voted affirmatively to do so, is guilty of blasphemy against the Word of God.

"What arrogance you display as you degenerate and set yourselves up as re-interpreters of the Holy Scriptures! Read the account of Genesis *one* more time. Man was created in the image of God. Do you interpret this to mean God is a homosexual? When the Bible states that 'Adam knew his wife, Eve' do you interpret this to mean that Eve was male and that sodomy began with Adam? Hardly—since Eve conceived. She didn't conceive through an act of sodomy, sir.

"Homosexuality is the result of man's sin. To say that males or females are born to be homosexual is really saying that God has erred. That my friend, is blasphemy at its worst!!

"All sin, except blasphemy against the Holy Scripture, is forgivable. By putting your 'blessing' on homosexual unions, you are giving legitimacy to sin. How incredibly sad.

"Perhaps you had better practice what you'll say to our Heavenly Father when you are called upon to explain your actions."—Chapel Hill, N.C.

"Although I am no longer involved in the Baptist Church," wrote one woman, "I still receive our state Baptist newspaper where I learned of your church's decision. I applaud and admire you for taking such a step in the face of what must be incredible opposition. By acknowledging, accepting, and affirming the love and commitment of these two people, you are expressing the inclusive love of God for all people. . . .

"I left the Southern Baptist denomination last fall after having been actively involved in many levels of Baptist life for 23 years. My decision to leave was based on several reasons, but one of the most painful was knowing that, though I had served the church in many capacities over the years, I would no longer be accepted if my sexual orientation were known."

"You are a symbol of hope to me, because you are willing to trust one another enough to engage in the discussion of homosexuality. . . . That your current struggle with the issue of human love has produced open and

honest encounter among persons in your congregation moves me deeply."—
retired minister, United Church of Christ.

News that the union had actually transpired brought an outpouring of
letters to the congregation of Pullen. All told, the correspondence from
individuals was about evenly divided between those expressing support
and those expressing outrage. The letters from other Southern Baptist
churches, however, were almost universal in their condemnation of the
ceremony.

The Baptist churches' letters all adhered to the same basic format. They
began with a statement supporting the Baptist tradition of local church
autonomy—the right of each congregation to make the decisions for its
church. But each letter concluded with a reason why this particular action
was different, and deserving of special censure—in essence saying that
Pullen had the right to make its own decision on this matter, but only if
it made the correct decision. Many of the churches that wrote seemed
concerned about the public relations fallout from the union ceremony.

"As Baptists, we feel this particular action is bad for the image of our
denomination," wrote one North Carolina church.

Another concurred: "Your church, in it's condonement of homosexuality, has severely damaged the witness of other Baptist churches in the
eyes of unbelievers. Surely your actions have cast in the minds and hearts
of Christians everywhere a cloud of doubt, uncertainty, and mistrust in
the Baptist Faith."

One of the state associations demanded a retraction: "We further believe
that your action has brought a reproach on the name of Jesus Christ and
Southern Baptists as a denomination. We request of you that this action
be rescinded and evidence of repentance for this action be shown in the
secular press as well as our Baptist newspaper."

Some of the churches went so far as to state what would happen if
Pullen did not comply with their demands: "In my opinion your church
should withdraw from the Raleigh Baptist Association, the North Carolina
Baptist Convention, and the Southern Baptist Convention. If you choose
not to withdraw, we strongly urge our Convention to take proper steps
to remove your church from our fellowship."

Ironically, the most articulate defense of Pullen's decision came from Mike

Watts, who had ultimately decided to vote against performing the union. A lifelong Baptist, Mike Watts was desperately concerned that his church's decision would lead to its expulsion from the Southern Baptist Convention. After the union ceremony, he even went so far as to introduce a motion reversing Pullen's position and forbidding it from doing any more same-sex unions. In spite of Mike's efforts to drum up support for it, that motion never passed.

But although Mike was firmly opposed to the union, he also felt that it was something that the members of the church could "agree to disagree" about—and that they should look beyond this one issue and remember the value of their fellowship. This attitude was a particularly healthy one for a man in Mike's position: both his wife and daughter had voted in favor of the union.

Mike understood the scriptural arguments for and against the union very clearly. He holds degrees in divinity and theology, and was once a Baptist preacher. A bout of Hong Kong flu ravaged his vocal chords, however, leaving him with a high squeaky voice that would simply never carry in church. As a result, Mike had gotten in the habit of doing some of his best arguing in writing.

In a letter to a fundamentalist friend, Mike attempted to explain how Pullen arrived at its decision. He never supported the outcome, but he did want to show how reasonable Bible-following Christians could have voted as the members of Pullen did, and why their decision should be tolerated by other Baptists.

Mike began by analyzing the Old Testament. There were only three references to homosexuality that he could find, and one of those was pretty clearly a prohibition on the use of temple prostitutes. As for the other two:

> The description of an apparent homosexual act in Leviticus 18:22 is translated into the *hetero*-sexual terminology of the time and somewhat euphemistically. It is addressed to *males* (as the entire law was—females were not often seen as objects of God's attention, being mere "possessions" of their fathers or their husbands). This verse reads: "Do not lie with a male as one lies with a woman; it is an abhorrence." (Jewish Publication Society Translation, 1985). No explanation is given as to just *why* it is such an abomination, and strangely, "lesbian" sexual activity is not mentioned here, nor anywhere else in the Old Testament. It is also

interesting to note that this prohibition of an apparent male homosexual act is not singled out as any more abhorrent than others, but appears in the middle of a *list* of other sexual acts which were considered "unclean," such as forbidden degrees of relationship (incest), and having sexual relations during a woman's monthly period of menstruation (Leviticus 18:19), a practice which people do not generally consider sinful in our society.

Leviticus 20:13 expands chapter 18's prohibition by applying the death penalty for the act condemned in 18:22. "If a man lies with another male as with a woman, the two of them have done an abhorrent thing; they shall be put to death—their bloodguilt is upon them." (JPS translation). In this same list the death penalty is prescribed for incest, adultery, lack of virginity in a woman on her wedding night, and for anyone who curses his father or mother! . . . It is interesting how selective we can be in our enforcement of scriptural "mandates," when *all* of these activities are treated on the *same* level in the Old Testament.

More important, at least from Mike's point of view, was the fact that modern Christians don't follow the laws of the Old Testament anyway. Or at best, they follow them only when it's convenient.

If it were not so, all Christians would worship on Saturday, as do the Jews, for there is no way to avoid the clear teaching of the Old Testament that the day of rest is the seventh day, not the first. If it were not so, all Christians would not be eating pork or shrimp, which are among the many forbidden foods in Jewish Law.

It is obvious that, for a majority of Christians, *not* all laws in the Old Testament have the same value. Christians usually refer to the words of Paul that "We are not under law, but under grace," when defending their failure to observe the Jewish Sabbath or the Jewish dietary laws. But then with a wonderful inconsistency, they quote Jesus, "I came not to destroy the Law, but to fulfill it," and "Not a jot nor a tittle of the Law shall disappear until all is fulfilled" when they come to a law like the condemnation of homosexuality that they believe is still valid. Paul reminded his readers that they could *not* have it *both* ways. Either a person must observe *all* of the Law in *all* of its details, or else he must be *free* from the Law and live under grace instead. Some in Christianity have not heard him on this point.

Mike went on to examine the New Testament.

In the first place, Jesus said *nothing* about homosexuality. . . . To argue from silence either to condemn or to condone may be possible, but the interpreter is always on shaky ground when arguing from silence. . . . The only references in the New Testament which may speak of homosexual activity are in the writings attributed to Paul.

Mike then cites the two references to "sodomites" in the writings of Paul, which appear to be fairly clear condemnations of homosexuality. But then Mike points out that "sodomites" is a dubious translation of a little-understood word in ancient Greek.

In these passages certain words are used which may or may not refer to what we know today as "homosexuality." The Greek word *pornos* (plural, *pornoi*) means "prostitute," and can refer to persons either heterosexual or homosexual. The Greek word *arsenokoites* (plural, *arsenokoitai*) is almost too ambiguous to translate. It comes from the word *Arsene*, "male," and the word *koite*, "bed." . . . *Malakos*, translated literally, means "soft" as in Matthew 11:8; in the passage in I Corinthians it suggests the idea of "effeminate," and could refer to a male prostitute who is a cross-dresser.

Again, before we attempt to apply these texts to twentieth century culture, it may be helpful to look at the culture of the Roman/Greek world of Mediterranean culture in the first century into which Christianity entered. In that culture there was in fact a very common form of same-sex activity which is often described in the literature of that period. It consisted of man-boy relationships in which men took pre-pubescent boys for sexual lovers. These men, often married men, provided an education and training for these boys, who were often slaves. . . . There were also male prostitutes in that society, many of whom dressed up as women with powder and makeup and perfume and who stood along the streets of places like Rome and Corinth selling themselves as did the female prostitutes. Again, while homosexuality as it exists in twentieth century society may have been present, it was probably not the dominant form, as it is not mentioned to any great extent in the literature of the period. And the idea of permanent monogamous same-gender relationships such as has been in question in recent news events was *not* really a part of the culture.

It is certainly clear from all the passages cited, when interpreted in the context of the cultural situations being addressed, that prostitution is condemned, that sexual abuse *is* being condemned, that *non*-consenting sexual relations are being condemned, pederasty—sexual exploitation of young boys—*is* being condemned. It is *less* certain that same-gender relationships between consenting adults are being condemned. There is certainly *no* evidence for "blessing" them, but the evidence for condemning them is not so certain either. That is as far as the Biblical evidence goes.

Thus, it appears, if one is to decide a Christian response to consenting homosexual activity, especially life-long monogamous same-gender relationships, it must be on more general grounds, rather than on the basis of those passages traditionally thought to refer to homosexuality. If we examine the actions and words of Jesus in the Gospels, however, it is clear that He was far more accepting of the real and the reputed shortcomings of the outcasts and "sinners" of his day than He was of those whose lives were spent in defining the "Will of God" for others, and in defending God's honor against "sinners." He ate and drank and socialized with the tax gatherers, the prostitutes, and the unwanted of society. He did not require that they be perfect for Him to love them or associate with Him or be accepted by Him.

The intent of all this is *not* to assert that these are the only ways a person can interpret these passages—Only that it *is* possible for a Christian to read these passages and see a totally different interpretation of them from that which has traditionally been given; and that given these assumptions, it was perfectly logical that Christians at Pullen *could* have voted the way they did.[5]

The condemnations from other Baptist churches continued pouring in throughout March and April. On May 5, 1992, the Raleigh Baptist Association, the next level of Baptist organization after the local church, met to discuss the issue of Pullen's continued membership.

Eleven people from Pullen went to the meeting. Some of them had supported the union, some of them had opposed it, but they all wanted a chance to speak. They sought to explain how carefully Pullen had considered the issue, and why it had decided to perform the union. Most important, they wanted to explain why, right or wrong, it was Pullen's right to make this decision for itself. They were never given the chance.

At the start of the meeting, the moderator announced that each speaker would be limited to three minutes. This immediately caused a stir from some of the more moderate representatives from other churches. They pointed out that three minutes was too short a time to say much of anything, and moved that Pullen be given fifteen minutes to state its case at the beginning of the meeting. This suggestion was voted down. The same representatives stood up again, and motioned that Pullen be given at least ten minutes to speak. This motion was voted down as well, this time amid open laughter from its opponents.

As the pastor of Pullen, Reverend Siler was granted the right to speak first. Exactly three minutes into his speech, members of the association began shouting "time," and the moderator ordered him to sit down. No other member of Pullen was allowed to speak during the course of the evening. Although the moderator had made a promise of equal time for both sides, it rapidly became clear that he had no intention of honoring it. One delegate from another church objected to this obvious railroading and stood up. When she was recognized to speak, she turned and yielded her three minutes to Reverend Siler, so that he could continue his speech. She was immediately ruled out of order and told to sit down.[6]

The eleven members of Pullen watched in disbelief as speaker after speaker denounced Pullen for its "un-Christian" stand and called for its expulsion, while they were given no chance to defend their church. "The tenor and mode of the meeting betrayed a rancor bordering on hate," Miriam Prichard wrote afterward. "For this we were not prepared." She continued: "If I could have spoken . . . I would have offered assurance that their Christian witness would not be besmirched by an example of kindness and largess. Rather, I would have said, perhaps the world would take heart at seeing a body of people continue to include and love and associate with others with whom they disagree. This is a witness that the world badly needs."[7]

The members of the Raleigh Baptist Association, however, did not see things that way. At the end of the meeting, Pullen was voted out of the association.

Mike Watts was infuriated by the whole process. As a conservative who had opposed the union, he shared many beliefs with the representatives who were now so angry with Pullen. And yet he hadn't even been granted the right to speak, to explain why he had stayed with Pullen in spite of the union and why he thought that the Raleigh Baptist Association should too.

"People ask me why the 36 percent [who voted against the union] don't just leave Pullen and break fellowship," Mike wrote in a letter to the

Raleigh News and Observer. "But our faith tells us that the power of love can transcend our differences. And where would we go, if we left? I saw on May 5 how dissenters are treated in other Raleigh churches. Compare that with my experience at Pullen.

"My voice and influence are very much alive there. I am not removed from committees. I still teach Sunday School. I freely write and post open letters to our members urging reconsideration of our vote. . . . I can't imagine having that kind of freedom in most of the congregations that excluded us.

"I regret the separation from our beloved Raleigh Baptists. But I revel in my freedom to dissent, and I sorrow that they have no such freedom."[8]

Several weeks later, Pullen provided Mike with a fitting demonstration of its tolerance for disagreement. Despite his continued minority stand against the union, Mike was elected a deacon of the church.

After the debacle in the Raleigh Baptist Association, it was clear that the North Carolina Baptist Convention and the Southern Baptist Convention would also expel Pullen. Another Baptist church, Binkley Memorial, had also taken a controversial stand on homosexuality over an altogether different issue. Now the conventions wanted to get rid of both of them. The executive committee of the North Carolina Baptist Convention announced that it had drafted an amendment to the charter, forever banning any church that supported homosexuality from belonging to the convention.

There were a number of Baptists, both conservative and moderate, who balked at this when it was proposed. Whatever their feelings about homosexuality, this was a clear attempt by the executive committee to impose dogma on the member churches, in direct violation of the Baptist doctrine supporting the autonomy of the individual church. C. Fred Werhan, who sat on the state convention's General Board, sent a letter to his fellow board members outlining the dangers of what they were considering. He said in part: "However strongly you may feel about the issue of homosexuality, or however right you may be in your understanding and position against it, once you, by this proposed action, impose your views upon others as a test of fellowship, you have violated the very freedom which characterizes us as Baptists. Being Baptists, more than anything else, means 'Freedom' . . . even the freedom to be wrong sometimes, which Baptists have been many times."[9]

In the end, such concerns fell on deaf ears. At the state convention, Pullen was once again prevented from even speaking in defense of its actions. Both Pullen and Binkley were expelled. That June they were expelled from the Southern Baptist Convention as well.

What did all of this mean for Pullen? The congregation wasn't too happy about being thrown out of the fold, to be sure, but it certainly didn't make the members change their minds. Newell Tarrant, an eighty-one-year-old member, told one reporter, "We all regret it [the expulsion], but I think we were right and we'll stick with it. We're Baptists and this has been Baptist for centuries—the right of the individual church to govern itself."[10] It seems that there are still some Baptists out there who agree with him. Another large Baptist denomination, the American Baptist Churches USA, for example, continues to welcome Pullen as one of its member churches.

All told, Pullen lost more than fifteen families over the course of the conflict. In the end, however, most of those who voted against the union decided to stay with the church. Even though their views hadn't prevailed this time, they still felt that their opinions were respected. Allen Paige, a member for twenty years, summed up the feeling. "Some people feel the community is more important than a single issue."[11]

Mike Watts's Sunday school class, consisting mostly of older, more conservative members, was particularly hard hit by the exodus. It dropped from twenty-five attenders a week down to about ten. In a letter to Pat Long, his opponent in much of the debate, Mike talked about what he felt had been lost and gained in the struggle over the union.

"My grief that the motion passed, I hope you understand, was primarily a grief due to the loss of fellowship with fellow Southern Baptists, both within Pullen and outside. But in the midst of my grief over the losses, I have come to know people in Pullen that I never knew before, and on a much more intimate level. In contacts with people on all sides of the same-gender union issue, there has been more baring of souls, more honest seeking for the will of God, more pure Christian love and fellowship, than I have ever experienced. I feel closer to the heartbeat of this

church than I ever did before—not so much because I am a deacon—
. . . but because I have come to know so many people on a gut-level
whom I did not know before."[12]

Pullen remains a stable and unified church. The families who left have
been replaced by a number of new gay and lesbian members, who have
supported the church with both time and money. Although a few people
worried about a "gay takeover" of the church, those fears have mostly
faded as the new members have blended into the existing congregation.
The only change that an outsider might notice is that one occasionally
sees members of the same gender holding hands during services.

Over the next few years, Pullen performed two more same-sex unions,
with little controversy. In the summer of 1993 Pat Long celebrated her
union with her lover, Rebecca. Mike Watts, despite all his publicly stated
feelings on the matter, attended their ceremony and rejoiced for them. As
he explained to Pat, "I am not yet sure that I believe in *this*, but I believe
in *you*." A third union ceremony, also between two women, took place in
the fall of 1994.

Unfortunately, marriages, gay or straight, have never come with guar-
antees. In November of 1994 Pullen's first gay union came to an end,
when Kevin Turner and Steven Churchill separated.

CHAPTER 3

License to Preach: Binkley Baptist

Chapel Hill, North Carolina, 1992. "Relax, you're among friends." Those were the first words anyone said to John Blevins when he got to the church on that rainy evening in January. He'd arrived a good twenty minutes before the meeting was set to start, so there were only a couple of other people standing around. John helped them set up folding chairs for the large group they were expecting, and tried not to get nervous about the big event coming up. Gradually, the deacons and the lay members began filtering in. A few of them walked over to John to wish him luck and to tell him not to worry.

And then, at 7:30, one of the deacons called the meeting to order and things got under way. John stood up and led the group in prayer. Then he proceeded to tell a congregation of Southern Baptists what it was like to be gay and why he felt called to be a minister.

It had all started nine months earlier, on April 8, 1991, at a meeting of the Board of Deacons of Olin T. Binkley Memorial Baptist Church. That's when Linda Jordan, the head minister, had presented John Blevins and Anne Marie Marshbanks as candidates to be licensed to preach the gospel. Licensure is the first step in becoming a Baptist minister. It requires the approval of the candidate's congregation and represents their belief in his or her sincerity and commitment to the ministry. For second-year divinity students like John and Anne Marie, there is generally little question of their commitment, and licensure is a routine matter. Anne Marie was interviewed once by a panel of deacons and then licensed at the next regular meeting of the board. Simple enough. The decision about John would be a bit more complicated, for two reasons. First, John is gay. Second, he said so to the deacons.

John had come out of the closet during his first year at Duke's Divinity School. It had been a difficult decision. Certainly, his chances for ordination would have been a lot better if he had kept his mouth shut. But to John, the whole issue boiled down to the simple question of whether or not he was going to be an honest person. Maybe it made sense for gay lawyers or politicians to hide their sexuality to protect their jobs. But the ministry is supposed to be not a job, but a calling. If you're not going to stand up for the truth, regardless of the cost, then what is the point of becoming a minister in the first place? In the end, the idea of getting into the ministry by lying was too much for John. He discussed his sexuality with a number of people at Binkley, including his minister. And when it came time for the deacons to render their decision on his licensure, he made sure that they knew who he really was.

At most Southern Baptist churches, given the conservative nature of the denomination, John's application would have been thrown out immediately. But Binkley, like Pullen, had a history of challenging traditions. From its founding in 1955 Binkley had been a racially integrated congregation, and it had played an active role in the civil rights movement. More recently it had raised eyebrows among the leaders of the Southern Baptist Convention by hiring a woman to be its head minister. (Indeed, some conservative members within Binkley were still grumbling about that move.) Binkley too was a congregation that was accustomed to tackling issues—racial equality, women's rights, the peace movement—years before most other Southern Baptist churches would even talk about them. Nevertheless, John's request was unprecedented.

The three deacons who interviewed John were united in finding that he had a sincere calling to the ministry. They were divided, however, on the role that his sexuality should play in their decision. Byron McCane, the chair of the interview committee, argued that being gay made John inherently unsuitable for the ministry. But the other two deacons felt that if God had truly called John to the ministry, then God's will needed to be respected and accepted.

When the interview committee reported back, they discovered that the rest of the diaconate was divided over the issue as well. After some debate, it became clear that the matter would not be easily settled. The deacons were able to agree on what they should do next, however. As at Pullen, the board decided that there was only one reasonable course of action for a democratic church which held to the idea of the priesthood of the believer—they would let the congregation as a whole debate the matter, discuss it, and eventually vote on it.

The deacons realized that this would be a singularly important vote. Not only would it have a major impact on John's life, but there could be severe repercussions for the church as well. If Binkley was going to make a decision this important, then the deacons wanted to make sure that it was a well-informed one. The deacons set aside six months to educate themselves and the congregation about every aspect of homosexuality, from current scientific theories of its cause to biblical debates over its sinfulness.

The deacons began by putting together a bibliography of useful readings on homosexuality. As with everything they did, they attempted to choose material from both sides of the issue. They obtained many of the readings for Binkley's library, and placed them where they would be easy to find. For those who didn't have time to do a lot of reading on the subject, the deacons put together a packet of short articles and mailed them to every member of the congregation. The packet contained information on recent scientific theories about a genetic cause for homosexuality, theological theories about why homosexuality was sinful, and finally, a written debate between two of the deacons—one who supported Blevins's licensure and one who was against it.

The deacons attempted to set up some live debates as well. Several speakers, including Reverend Siler of Pullen Baptist and Furman Hewitt, a former professor at Southeastern Baptist Seminary, argued that the Church needed to reconsider its traditional stand on homosexuality and that Binkley should evaluate Blevins on his abilities as a minister, not on his sexuality. The diaconate had great difficulty, however, finding anyone who was willing to speak publicly against Blevins's licensure. The diaconate invited Richard Hays, a New Testament scholar who has written extensively on the letters of Paul and who is frequently quoted by those who wish to prove that the Bible condemns homosexuality. But Hays declined their invitation to speak, and no substitute would agree to take his place. After several more unsuccessful tries to line up a speaker, the diaconate assigned an assistant pastor to read from Hays's work at a church meeting and to summarize his arguments on the sinfulness of homosexuality.

In private discussions, Byron McCane, who was lobbying heavily against John's licensure, would point to the lack of opposition speakers as evidence that the diaconate was not serious about trying to present both sides of the issue—obviously they were trying to muzzle the conservatives. McCane's argument, however, was a bit disingenuous, since he himself had turned down two invitations from the diaconate to speak against the licensure and explain the conservative view.

That fall Binkley held a series of Sunday evening classes entitled "Living Values in Changing Times." The discussions were led by two licensed therapists and were designed to cover questions of spirituality and sexuality. The sessions were well attended. During one discussion on homosexuality, two openly gay members of the congregation came to discuss their experiences in the church. During another discussion on AIDS, the class was joined by one member of the church who was HIV positive.

Linda Jordan addressed the subject from the pulpit in a series of six sermons on a Christian approach to sexuality. And on Sunday, December 29, Blevins himself was allowed to preach. He stated that the congregation's decision would have to come "from God's call, and not from some social or political agenda." But he also pointed out the dangers of relying strictly on scriptural law to know the will of God: "As Psalm 119 says, it is a lamp which guides our steps and illuminates our way, never providing an all-consuming final light." Blevins illustrated his point by relating the story of another sexual outcast who had sought entrance to the church—the parable of the eunuch:

> The Ethiopian eunuch thirsted for God and sought to know who God was through the Scriptures. But the word of God was clear: a eunuch could not belong to the people of God (Deut. 23:1). That was the only printed "Law" Philip had to go by. There was no way that Philip could be faithful to that printed word and baptize the eunuch. The prohibition was undeniable. But Philip saw the law of God written on the eunuch's heart, and Philip accepted him into the kingdom. The eunuch's experience of God was true and real and Philip accepted it under the new covenant God put on the eunuch's heart.[1]

Byron McCane was also invited to speak from the pulpit on his views about the issue. He again declined. In fact, shortly after the education process began at Binkley, McCane resigned his membership in the church. His exact reasons for leaving Binkley remain unclear. He told some people that he was leaving to accept a job at another church, others that he was leaving because of all the blasphemous talk about homosexuality.

Even after leaving Binkley, though, McCane continued to lobby individual members of the church against Blevins's licensure. In phone calls and personal meetings, McCane argued that licensing Blevins would amount to an endorsement by Binkley of homosexuality, something he believed that the Bible universally condemned. Still, McCane was remarkably unwilling to articulate in public the views he was advocating in private. When interviewed, he refused even to say what side of the debate he was on, responding only that he was "disappointed with how politicized the process had become."[2]

It seems that while McCane did not want to see a homosexual licensed to preach the gospel, he also did not want to be seen as fighting against *John Blevins's* licensure. In many ways, John was a perfect candidate. People who had spoken with him were often impressed by his passion for the ministry. Furthermore, he was a very likable young man, and it was difficult for anyone to see him as a monster bent on destroying the church. McCane seems to have felt that arguing against Blevins personally would have made him appear mean-spirited and un-Christian. Indeed, the only public statement McCane ever made of his beliefs was a letter he composed for the information packet that the diaconate mailed out to the congregation. In it, McCane attacks homosexuality while bending over backward not to attack John.

McCane began the letter by attempting to explain why the Bible denounces homosexual behavior in the first place. "The Bible condemns homosexuality simply because of the doctrine of creation (Genesis 1–3), which says that God created male and female. Based on that teaching about creation, the Bible views homosexual behavior as a distortion of God's design. From a Biblical point of view, homosexual activity is similar to pollution of the environment: it is an activity whereby humans mar the beauty of God's created order."[3]

McCane then responded to recent scientific studies that suggested that homosexuality might be a genetically determined trait. As Byron saw it, genetics had nothing to do with whether a behavior was sinful or not. "As a result [of these studies], it is sometimes argued that homosexual orientation is virtually innate, and thus may not be morally bad. This conclusion, however, needs to be tempered by the realization that not all innate tendencies are good; some are quite bad (alcoholism), so the scientific account of homosexuality does not really solve the ethical and theological problem."[4]

McCane attacked the notion that homosexuals should be welcomed out of a desire to be inclusive—a belief that everyone has a place in God's church.

> Inclusiveness is not, and never has been, the Gospel of Christ; it is simply
> an ideal currently in vogue among a certain set of white liberals.
> Inclusiveness is, it seems to me, an idol of our culture which is in danger
> of becoming an idol in the church. The Gospel, by contrast, has always
> included a call to repentence from sin.
>
> So, to turn to the specific question faced by our Board, should John
> Blevins be licensed and ordained? After talking with John on several
> occasions, I believe the answer is Yes, because he clearly has the gifts and
> calling for the ministry. Should John be licensed and ordained in a way
> which affirms, celebrates, or legitimates his homosexuality? Each of us
> must decide that question in our own heart, but for my part, I believe
> that the answer is No.[5]

From this public statement, it was difficult to know whether McCane actually supported Blevins's licensure or not. In private, however, Byron told members of the congregation that since Blevins had brought up his sexuality before the church, there was now no way to license him without endorsing homosexuality.

Finally, on a rainy weekday night in January of 1992, the congregation called on John to answer their questions for himself. John began by telling them about the summer after his junior year in high school, when he first felt his calling to the ministry. He was at Baptist summer camp, and he remembers feeling "something happening. Something I needed to do. Something I had to do. Something I ought to do." At the time, John told no one about his feeling. He knew that emotions often ran high at

church camps, and that many of his friends would make promises then that
they would never follow up on. He didn't know if his own commitment
would outlast the summer. But it turned out to be a feeling that never left
him.

John also told the congregation about his struggle with homosexuality. By the time he received his call to the ministry, John had already realized
that he was attracted to other men. Blevins talked about his fear and frustration at not being able to ask anyone for help, knowing that even
admitting what he felt would make him an outcast. John spoke of the
times that he prayed to God to remove this attraction, to heal it. He also
spoke of the time, years later, when he finally came to accept it, to see it
as a natural part of himself; when he realized that God hadn't "fixed it"
because it had never been broken in the first place.

Several members of the congregation asked John about the biblical
prohibitions on homosexual acts. John admitted that they seemed to be
clear. But he also pointed to the times in the past when Scripture had been
used to justify unjust behavior. For decades, the Southern Baptist church
had quoted the letters of Paul to prove that slavery was a moral practice
endorsed by heaven. Even now, many Southern Baptists used Paul's words
to prove that God wanted women to be quiet and submissive to men. Should
we accept Paul's words, he asked, and go back to the days of slavery? Or
should we instead take a look at what is going on in our world and ask
how a loving and fair God would have us act: with compassion, or with
bigotry?

One member asked Blevins why he was seeking licensure from a Southern
Baptist church. He had to know that it would be a difficult process.
Wouldn't things be easier if John switched to the Unitarian church, which
had no qualms about ordaining homosexuals? John said that he had considered such a move. But when it came right down to it, he wasn't a
Unitarian. He had been raised in the Southern Baptist church, and deep
down he believed in the basic tenets of the Baptist faith, including the
priesthood of the believer and the autonomy of the local church. John
was seeking to be ordained in the Baptist church for the simple reason
that he was a Baptist.

Another member of the congregation asked if John thought that a gay
minister could be a good role model for children. John answered the
unspoken part of that question by saying that he didn't think seeing a gay

minister would lead a child to become a homosexual. "After all, a heterosexual minister didn't cause me to be straight." But, John pointed out, the congregation needed to accept the fact that some of its children were going to grow up to be gay. Having a gay minister to talk with, and a church that accepted them, might make those children's lives much easier. The church could help them come to terms with their sexuality and encourage them to use it in a responsible and loving way.

Others were more interested in knowing how John was using his own sexuality. Knowing that he had a boyfriend, they asked if John was a "potential" homosexual or a "practicing" homosexual. John admitted that he was of the "practicing" variety. At this point one speaker asked how John could possibly be ordained since he had just confessed to engaging in premarital sex. John respectfully pointed out that since Binkley was not yet willing to perform same-sex weddings, it was unfair to condemn him for not being married. Indeed, John very much wanted to be married. He was in a loving, committed relationship, and hoped that it would last a very long time.

Finally, there were several members who were concerned about the consequences for Binkley itself if it licensed John. They pointed out that one deacon had already left the church over the issue, and they expressed the fear that other members might do the same. They asked John if his licensure was really worth the division it was causing in the congregation.

John responded by saying that the division on the issue of homosexuality had been there long before he ever joined Binkley. He was simply bringing it to the surface where it could be discussed, debated, and, he hoped, healed. "The Church has got to deal with this issue," he said. "It's not going to go away. There are a lot of people who already feel alienated from the Church. Will we reach out to them, or take the easy route by denying them?"

On February 3, the diaconate met to vote on its recommendation to the congregation. Four of them chose to miss the meeting. One abstained. Seven voted to recommend against Blevins's licensure. Fifteen voted in favor of it. The results were reported in Binkley's newsletter, and the Church Council scheduled a congregational meeting for April 5 to conduct the final vote on the matter.

On February 15, Richard Jenkins posted a letter resigning his member-ship in Binkley Baptist. "Those churches which attempt to include everyone," he wrote, "often end up including very few. Growing churches and denominations are those which have been willing to set limits and to to proclaim 'Thus saith the Lord.' " In his letter, Jenkins argued that there was a conspiracy among the leaders of the church to force the con-gregation into accepting homosexuality. Like Byron McCane, he cited the lack of opposition speakers as proof that the diaconate was not truly studying both sides of the issue. As he saw it, the entire education process had been "designed to desensitize church members to alternative sexu-alities."[6]

There was a grain of truth to Jenkins's charges. Although the diaconate, whose members were divided over the issue themselves, had been careful to present both sides of the matter, it was becoming clear that the education process was having the effect of moving many members toward endorsing Blevins's licensure. The more they talked about homosexuality, the less alien and frightening it became. In the last weeks before the April 5 vote, it became increasingly clear that the congregation was going to decide in favor of licensing John Blevins.

As support for the licensure grew, so did conservative charges of a pro-homosexual conspiracy. In the eyes of the conservatives, since education was moving the congregation toward acceptance of homosexuality, that education must somehow be biased. As it became obvious that they were going to lose the vote, the conservatives began referring to the education program with terms such as "programming" and "indoctrination."

On March 17, the opposing sides on the diaconate put out a statement of their positions on Blevins's licensure. The statement summarized the arguments for and against the move.

In Favor of the Recommendation
   1. We believe that John has been called by God to the Christian ministry. He is a qualified candidate for the ministry by the accepted edu-cational standards. Licensure simply recognizes John's qualifications and Call, and our congregation's support of his pilgrimage of ministry.
   2. Binkley Church has long accepted homosexuals into full member-ship and church life. Once a person is baptized, that person is a full

member of the community of faith. There should be no restrictions on that person's services to the community in response to the Lord's Call.

3. The scriptural testimony on homosexuality condemns abusive and/or exploitive sexual behavior. Jesus did not speak on the issue of homosexuality. The overall Biblical message is one of love.

4. Christian faith compels us to examine church tradition in the light of new evidence. The present state of knowledge and insight can no longer sufficiently support the unqualified condemnation of all homosexual practice.

5. Homosexuality can be practiced within an intimate relationship which expresses the love, respect, mutuality, and commitment possible in a heterosexual relationship. When practiced in this way, homosexuality can be life-affirming and harms neither individuals nor the community.

Opposed to the Recommendation

1. The Scriptures speak clearly to the point that homosexual behavior is sinful. The creation story, Biblical teaching about marriage, and specific admonitions against homosexuality support this position. Specific Scripture references include Genesis 1–2, Romans 1, and I Corinthians 6–9.

2. Intimate sexual activity outside of marriage is immoral, regardless of sexual orientation, and renders a candidate unsuitable for licensure.

3. A practicing homosexual is an inappropriate role model as a minister.

4. While we celebrate the inclusive nature of our congregation, being inclusive does not require approval of sinful behavior. In the same way, moral disapproval cannot be equated with having a lack of love, acceptance, or regard for civil rights and social justice.

5. The traditional teaching of the Christian Church for 2000 years opposes the practice of homosexuality. There is not sufficient evidence to abandon this position.

6. The fact that homosexuality might be caused by factors beyond a person's control does not mean that the practice of homosexuality ought to be affirmed.

7. To affirm and accept a request for licensure by a homosexual is to accept and affirm homosexuality—a position we cannot accept.[7]

In the last two weeks before the congregational vote, the church had meetings every Tuesday and Sunday night. Attendance varied from as low as ten to as high as two hundred. Most of the people at the meetings spoke in favor of Blevins's licensure, and it seemed that the church was coming to a consensus on the issue. One person, who knew the statistic that one in ten men is gay, pointed out: "The Lord had twelve disciples, and chances are that one of them was gay."[8]

As the final vote approached, the opposition to Blevins's licensure grew more desperate. Conservative members posted a flurry of letters to the diaconate, protesting that the congregation had not had enough time to adequately consider the matter, and that therefore the vote should be postponed for a lengthy period. Because John was graduating in June, and presumably moving away to seek a job, delaying the vote long enough would have the effect of removing the question from consideration altogether. The diaconate responded to these letters by pointing out that the matter had already been under consideration for nearly a year, and that a poll taken several weeks earlier showed that a majority of the congregation had been following the issue closely and was now ready to vote on it. The final vote would take place April 5 as scheduled.

Those last weeks before the vote were not an easy time for Blevins. There were times when John felt as if he had ceased to be a person and had become only a political issue. As he put it at one meeting, "I feel that I am being talked about and not talked to."[9]

On April 5, the congregation gathered to cast its final vote on the matter. There was a great deal of last-minute debate, and the meeting dragged on for several hours.

John Humber introduced a motion to delay the vote until Binkley had established an official policy on homosexuality. Humber argued that it was unfair to make people vote against Blevins personally. Instead, they should be able to vote on whether *any* homosexual could be licensed, without getting into the specifics of Blevins's case. This motion was widely regarded as a stalling tactic, and was voted down. A second motion, to adjourn the meeting because it was getting late and to vote on the matter another time, was similarly defeated.

On the other side of the issue, Jim Wilde offered an amendment to the motion for Blevins's licensure. It was a long amendment, full of praise for God and quotes from Scripture, which sought to meet Humber's demand for an official church policy on homosexuality. It was not, however, the policy which Humber would have wished for. Instead, it read in part:

"The Olin T. Binkley Memorial Baptist Church, when it calls persons to pastoral leadership and when it considers requests for licensure or ordination to the Christian ministry, shall disregard the sexual orientation of those under consideration." The wording was accepted as a friendly amendment into the motion for licensure.

Finally, late in the evening, the matter was put to a vote. By this time, 14 members of the congregation had had to leave. The final vote was 145 in favor to 107 opposed. It had taken a year, but John Blevins was now officially licensed to preach the gospel.

"The lack of concern," wrote Leslie Coggins in a letter to the *Chapel Hill News*, "of the people who pushed the vote on John Blevins to the other 300 members of the church (about half were present the night of the vote) was what finally made us realize that this was not a loving congregation. No one had reached out to us, and the political power struggle that resulted in the licensure decision (the gross misuse of power entrusted by others in the boards) forced the immediate move to become inactive and withdraw financial support.

"Unfortunately, this experience has scarred me deeply. I find it hard to go to church because I dread the possibility of something like this going on again. The trust I used to have in church people has simply turned to distrust. . . . I doubt that I will ever have that trusting nature again."[10]

At Pullen Baptist, the conservatives had not been happy about their loss. Still, they had felt that the process had been fair, that the church had listened to their opinions, and that they would probably find themselves on the winning side of other arguments in the future. Although they didn't agree with the decision that was reached, they could see how reasonable Christians could disagree about such an issue. At Pullen, both sides seemed to agree that the church was bigger than this single issue.

It did not work out that way at Binkley. The conservatives did not feel that Blevins's licensure was a matter about which they could simply "agree to disagree." Indeed, they referred to the vote in quite apocalyptic terms, as "the loss of the church" or "the destruction of the church."[11] In their view, opposition to homosexuality was an integral part of the Christian message, and any church that ceased to preach this was no longer following God's will. It is never easy to lose when you believe that you are fighting for a moral principle, and the conservatives at Binkley were particularly stung. As the defeated opposition saw it, their cause had been just. They felt they could not have lost unless the other side had resorted to treachery and deception.

Three of the opposition deacons called a meeting on May 3 for all the members of the church who had voted against the licensure. Humber, one of the participants in the meeting, described it: "Some forty persons attended and for three hours they listened to each other, to their feelings of anger and betrayal, of sorrow and frustration over the virtual destruction of their church."[12] The more the group discussed the matter, the more they came to believe that there had been a conspiracy to lead the church away from God. After all, how could so many God-fearing people have voted to license a homosexual unless someone had deliberately misled them? Those at the meeting convinced themselves that the congregation at Binkley had not truly voted in favor of Blevins's licensure. After all, a number of people had not attended the meeting, and there was no way of knowing how they would have voted. The key now was somehow to undo Blevins's licensure. Surely, if they had more time to make the congregation see reason, and if they used absentee ballots so that the entire church voted, they could defeat this radical measure once and for all.

The group decided to appeal to the Church Council to overturn the Wilde amendment, on the grounds that copies of it had not been distributed a week prior to the congregational meeting. Furthermore, they argued, any motion to which it was attached—namely, Blevins's licensure—should also be overturned. Everything would be turned back to the way that it had been before April 5, and all would be well. This time they wouldn't lose.

The matter was brought before the council on May 18. After consulting *Robert's Rules of Order* and Binkley's constitution, the council determined that nothing unconstitutional had taken place. The motion for Blevins's licensure had been distributed a week in advance of the meeting, and it was perfectly acceptable for amendments to be made from the floor without prior warning. Furthermore, any challenge to the amendment on distribution grounds should have been made on the evening of the congregational meeting, before the matter was put to a vote. As the council saw it, moreover, one simply didn't go around de-licensing people from preaching the gospel. The matter had been voted on, John had his license, and it was time to move on to other business. The licensure would stand.

The path got a bit rocky for Binkley after its decision to license John Blevins. The seven deacons who opposed the move have all quit the church, as did a number of lay members. Donations dropped by 15 percent, and the church budget had to be revised. John Humber self-published a booklet entitled "The Ordeal and Tragedy of Binkley Baptist Church," in which he detailed his charges of a pro-homosexual conspiracy within the church. And on June 9, 1992, the Southern Baptist Convention expelled Binkley along with Pullen. In so doing, the convention ended the long-standing Baptist tradition of autonomous churches, and issued the denomination's first decree of faith. From this point on, all Southern Baptist churches had to accept opposition to homosexuality as a part of their creed.

But Binkley has held together. It was never financially dependent on the Southern Baptist Convention, and it has maintained its ties to the American Baptist Churches USA. The church's finances have stabilized, and the majority of members from both sides of the licensure issue have chosen to stick it out. There remain occasional arguments and some hurt feelings on both sides, but for the most part things seem to be on the mend.

John Blevins was in a bit of a bind for a while. There are two steps in becoming a Baptist minister, licensure and ordination. Although John was now licensed, he could not be ordained until he had been hired for a ministerial position. It was obvious that he wouldn't find any work in the Southern Baptist denomination—any church that hired him would immediately be expelled from the convention. However, John did have hopes of being hired by an American Baptist church.

Late in the summer, John received an offer from the AIDS Pastoral Care Network in Chicago. They were looking for a chaplain to work with AIDS patients and their families. Taking the job would mean moving away from his family and friends, but John knew that he didn't really have a choice if he wanted to follow his calling—there aren't that many jobs for openly gay Baptist ministers.

Blevins worked at two hospitals in Chicago, with adult patients at one and with children at another. Like all work with terminal patients, the job could be overwhelming at times. John said, "Some days it's boring, some days it's hectic, some days it's engaging, some days it's draining, some days it's exhilarating." But he was glad to be doing it.

John's work with children was particularly challenging. Children's Memorial Hospital is a research study site, so the patients often have blood samples taken, measurements done, and a wide variety of medical procedures performed on them. For the children, it can be a frightening and confusing experience. To help relieve their anxiety, John engaged in "medical play" with them. The hospital provided dolls with IV lines, and the children practiced giving them shots, drawing blood, and changing their IV bags. John explained: "They feel that they can get some control over what's going on, so that it's not quite so foreign to them, and therefore not as scary." It was satisfying to know that he could take a little bit of the terror out of a child's life, that he could make sick children laugh and smile for a little while. Still, it was difficult to watch so many of them die.

John's ordination fell through in May of 1993. Although Grace Baptist Church in Chicago agreed to sponsor him for ordination, his application got hung up in regional politics. The regional ordination committee balked when they realized he was gay, and asked the American Baptist Family Council of Metro Chicago to rule on whether or not a homosexual could be admitted to the ordination process. The Family Council, however, was no longer meeting, because the executive minister had resigned. He had only been in office for six weeks, and had no interest in getting involved with the potential firestorm of ordaining a gay man.

That left John's application floating in limbo for several months. Finally, a minister who supported his ordination told John that it was unlikely ever to take place. "He said that he thought it would probably be about two years before a policy came out, and that it would likely be something akin to 'Don't ask, don't tell'—if you don't bring it up in your ordination paper, we won't ask. But if you decide to disclose it, then we'll have to deny ordination."

To John, the whole thing seemed ridiculous. Throughout both the licensure and the ordination processes, people seemed to be telling him that they wanted to be lied to. Finally, he called Reverend Jordan at Binkley. Blevins explained what had happened in Chicago, and asked if he could come back to be ordained at Binkley, which is in the American Baptists' Southern Region. John asked if Binkley was ready to sponsor him for ordination, or if the scars from the licensure battle were too fresh.

On the phone, Reverend Jordan told him that it would be no problem:

And toward the end of that, I decided that I felt a call to the ordained ministry."

Richard entered Duke's Divinity School in the fall of 1989, the same year as John Blevins. Divinity school isn't the safest place to announce one's homosexuality, so for the first several weeks they told only their close friends. During the first month, neither of them knew about the other. In fact, Richard had pegged John as a conservative Southern Baptist, probably a fundamentalist. When John suggested that they have dinner to discuss something of importance, Richard expected it to be yet another lecture on how he could become straight through Christ. Instead, he was pleased and surprised to find a gay friend in his program.

The Divinity School was not an easy place for either of them to be gay. When John discussed his sexuality in a personal essay for Bill Turner's class, the professor told him in no uncertain terms that he should drop out of school. But because Duke's Board of Trustees had expanded the university's nondiscrimination clause to include sexual orientation several years earlier, there was nothing Turner could do to enforce this suggestion. He did, though, point out that John was wasting his time—no denomination would ever ordain a homosexual. Besides, if John would just open his heart, the Holy Spirit would heal him of this unnatural affliction. To John, who had prayed repeatedly for healing, this seemed to be a singularly uninformed piece of advice.

As time went by, both John and Richard became a little bolder in questioning their professors' condemnation of gay men and lesbians. One class they both attended was on sexual ethics, taught by Harmon Smith. During one session, Smith referred in passing to the promiscuity of the "gay lifestyle." Rather than letting it pass, John stopped to question him about it.

"I said, 'Well, if that really is a legitimate concern of yours, then one of the things the Church could do would be to help support and underwrite committed relationships, rather than denying their existence.'

"At that point he got really angry at me and said, 'You have no right to ask me that! No one is asking us to bring kleptomaniacs up to the front of the church and say, "Go ahead, we affirm you in your compulsion to steal!" ' "

In another session, on sexually transmitted diseases, Smith complained about how much money was being wasted on AIDS research. As he saw it, a lot more people had died of heart disease over the years than had ever succumbed to AIDS. Richard pointed out what a meaningless statistic that was—heart disease had been around for centuries before AIDS, and it was not spreading at the dangerous rate that AIDS was. John observed that since Smith had experienced a heart attack several years before, it was understandable that he would want more research devoted to that subject. If he were HIV positive, maybe he would feel differently about money being spent to cure AIDS.

In their second year of the program, Richard and John decided that they needed to do something to help change the homophobic atmosphere at the Divinity School, something that would educate both the students and the faculty. By this time they had connected with two other gay students in the program—Chuck Stanford, an Episcopalian, and Mike, a Methodist. The four signed their names to a flyer announcing the formation of a new student organization, Divinity Students for Gay and Lesbian Concerns (DSGLC).

It was an uphill battle from the beginning. To be recognized by the school, the new group needed a faculty sponsor. Although the group talked with several sympathetic professors, they were all junior faculty members and afraid that associating with DSGLC would ruin their chances for tenure. The group finally got lucky when they talked with Mary McClintock Fulkerson. Even though she was also a member of the junior faculty, she felt strongly about the need for a such a group and agreed to stick her neck out for them. Still, Mary told them that she could use a little cover—a co-sponsor with tenure who could take some of the heat off her.

Eventually Stanley Hauerwas, who taught ethics, agreed to fill that role. A full professor in both the Law School and the Divinity School, Hauerwas was well respected at Duke. Although he had no special interest in the group and never attended any of its meetings, Hauerwas felt that the subject needed to be discussed and allowed DSGLC to use his name.

Reactions to the new group were mixed. A number of closeted gay and lesbian students turned up for the meetings, as well as an even larger number of straight students who were simply curious. There was also, however, a violent and mostly anonymous backlash. Advertisements for DSGLC meetings were ripped off the school walls. Unsigned notes were stuffed in the mailboxes of the four students who had signed the first announcement. "Dick Bardusch. What would Freud say about a name like that?" John recalls, "There were snickers in the hallways, people turning their heads away, refusing to talk to us." An employee in the mail room started a petition to have DSGLC disbanded. And in one instance, signs went up around the school reading, "The Gospel according to Paul says that gay and lesbian alike should be excommunicated due to their character flaw." Presumably these posters were written by an outsider, since any divinity student would know that there is no Gospel according to Paul.

Mary McClintock Fulkerson was particularly upset by the anonymous nature of these attacks. While sitting in her office one afternoon, she heard someone walk up and rip an advertisement for the annual RRNGLE conference off her door. "The great noise made by the action alerted me that no small amount of feeling was being vented on my door," she wrote in a letter to the Divinity School's student paper. "It appears that there are some angry folks in the vicinity who would rather not discuss issues that unsettle them, and I don't believe there is a good theological or biblical precedent for that. I am hurt and disturbed that someone would destroy my property and—almost worse—miss an opportunity for Christian conversation. That someone could certainly be more prophetic in following her/his conscience if she/he *spoke for* the beliefs that prompted the action! I welcome opportunities to talk about the Gospel and issues pertaining to gayness—heterosexuality, too."[1]

Many people thought that the whole issue had been blown out of proportion. Jack Wallace, for example, worked in the Divinity School library alongside Richard Bardusch. The two talked about gay and lesbian issues on several occasions, although it quickly became clear that they agreed on very little. Still, Jack found the whole backlash against DSGLC ridiculous. There were more important things to be worrying about.

"I told Rich that I tried to look at the issue from a biblical perspective. . . . I think that if we want our preaching to be truly biblical we need to preach about that with which the Bible is truly concerned. You can count on one hand the verses which are concerned with homosexuality. It would take you all day to track down every verse concerning greed and the dangers of affluence. When was the last time you heard a sermon against making too much money?"[2]

As it turns out, some of those who were the most critical of DSGLC were in no position to be casting the first stone.

It is frequently claimed that the most homophobic people are themselves closeted homosexuals. One extreme example of this was Terry Thompson, another student in Duke's divinity program. Terry told his friends that he was absolutely against DSGLC, and that it had no business seeking funding from the student government. Like the women's group, which he also opposed, DSGLC served a special minority and wasn't of service to the student body as a whole. Terry was a conservative. Terry was a Methodist. Terry was also gay, and several men claim to have secretly dated him throughout his Divinity School career.

Terry never graduated, however. In a particularly bizarre incident, he shaved his head to mimic the effects of chemotherapy and began confiding to friends and professors that he was dying of a brain tumor. In one moving sermon delivered during his third year of the program, Terry told his classmates that his only wish was to live long enough to see graduation. Several of his classmates wept during the service. Afterward, he told many of them that his medical bills were more than he could manage. A number of students donated money to him, as did several parishioners from the Methodist church he attended.

Things began to unravel for Thompson when he told an administrator in the Divinity School about his medical problems. The administrator assured Terry that the school would cover all of his medical bills, if he would just provide them with copies. Several weeks later, the administrator began to wonder why Terry had not dropped off those copies of his bills, and took a walk across campus to make inquiries at Duke Medical Center.

It was then that the Divinity School discovered that Terry didn't have cancer, and never had. Terry was expelled, appropriately enough, on April Fools' Day, 1992. He disappeared before facing criminal charges for fraud and bouncing checks.[3]

Another interesting critic of the DSGLC was Paul Mickey, a Divinity School professor who taught pastoral care. Mickey wrote an entire book on the subject of homosexuality, entitled *Of Sacred Worth*. The text was an argument in support of the language of the Methodist *Book of Discipline*, which states that homosexuals are "people of sacred worth," but that they shouldn't be ordained and, further, that one cannot be both a practicing homosexual and a Christian. Mickey argued that the only moral course for homosexuals was to reject their sexual impulses and lead a celibate life. Mickey even went on television, appearing on the *700 Club* with Pat Robertson to promote his book.

Apparently, however, Paul Mickey felt that such rigorous sexual ethics were meant to apply to other people. Several months after his appearance with Pat Robertson, he was placed on permanent sabbatical by the Divinity School—essentially, he was fired. The school had discovered that Mickey, a married man, had been having an affair with one of his female students.

For both John and Richard, there were times when divinity school seemed like a crash course in hypocrisy. Many denominations have a written ban against the ordination of homosexuals, and these regulations have created a perverse situation. Those gay men who are honest about their sexuality and who have open, long-term relationships find it very difficult to become ministers. Those who are willing to lie face no obstacles. Thus it is often those who are the least ethical about their sex lives who are most easily ordained.

During Richard and John's time at Duke, one of the campus ministers was a closeted homosexual. This minister was in the habit of picking up male undergraduates in the library bathroom and persuading them to have unsafe sex. As one student described it, "He said that it was safe for him to fuck me without a condom as long as he pulled out in time." In some cases, these were students who would later be sent to him for counseling. But because this minister had never mentioned his sexuality in public, no one had ever bothered him about it and his ordination had sailed through without incident.

The four students who signed their names to the DSGLC announcement were hardly the only gay students in the divinity program. They were, however, the only ones who were honest with their classmates about it. And for that each of them would pay a price.

John would struggle for years to be ordained. Chuck would eventually drop out of divinity school. Mike would go back in the closet, and hope that people forgot. And Richard, an Episcopalian convert, would face some unique problems of his own.

In his second year of divinity school, Richard began the long process of applying for the Episcopal priesthood. One of the first steps is a psychiatric test to determine the candidate's emotional fitness.

In 1973 the American Psychiatric Association had removed homosexuality from its list of mental disorders. By then a number of scientific studies had shown that homosexuality did not in and of itself lead to antisocial or self-destructive behavior. In keeping with that research, the APA had relabeled homosexuality as a trait rather than a disease.

The particular psychiatrist employed by the local Episcopal diocese did not agree with that finding, however. Dr. Fred A. Vinson told Richard while he was taking the test, "If it was up to me, you wouldn't even be in this program."

But it was not up to Dr. Vinson. The psychiatrist's only responsibility was to administer the test and grade the results. As far as the test showed, there was nothing wrong with Richard. Still, Dr. Vinson made the most of his position. He forced Richard to make three separate trips to see him, to take the same five-hundred-question test over and over again. Each time, Richard asked the psychiatrist if he had found something wrong. Each time, the doctor said, "No, I just want to make sure."

Eventually, Dr. Vinson was forced to admit that Richard had indeed passed the test. His candidacy proceeded to the next step, his interview before the Commission on Ministry (COM). The COM is made up of clergy and lay members who ask the candidate a number of questions to make sure that he or she truly understands the demands of the priesthood. Some of the questions are standard and are asked of every candidate; others are chosen randomly. Occasionally, they ask candidates if they have ever had a gay experience. Richard was the first ever to answer "yes."

There was an awkward moment of silence, before one of the commission members thought to ask the next logical question. "Well, are you gay?"

Richard admitted that he was. From that point on, no other subject was discussed in his interview.

Not one member of the commission ever suggested to Richard that his sexuality was sinful or that it made him unsuitable for the priesthood.

Instead the discussion focused on how others would react to a gay priest. The COM pointed out that any church Richard could be assigned to was bound to have at least a few members with strong antigay feelings. Wouldn't that hinder his ministry?

Richard countered by arguing that an openly gay priest was exactly what some of these people needed. The best way to help people overcome fear or misconceptions about homosexuals is to let them get to know one. By serving as their priest, Richard could help those with antigay feelings work through their hatred and come to grips with it.

In the end the commission delayed Richard's application, but said that he could reapply the following year. They also made the question about homosexual experiences a standard part of the interview, to be asked of all future candidates for the priesthood.

The next year, his third and last in the divinity school, Richard went to Bishop Robert Estill and asked to begin the application process again. Bishop Estill responded by asking him a question.

"Will you promise not to practice?"

Richard thought about that for a moment. Finally, he said, "I can't do that."

"Then I cannot recommend you," said the bishop.

That effectively ended Richard's chances of being ordained.

In fairness to Bishop Estill, he was only following a resolution that was passed by the Episcopal General Convention in 1979. The resolution states that homosexuality is incompatible with Christian teaching, and forbids any bishop from ordaining a "practicing homosexual." This rule has been interpreted to mean that any gay or lesbian candidate for the priesthood must first take a vow of celibacy. Some Episcopalians have defended this requirement by saying that they are asking no more of homosexuals than they ask of their heterosexual priests—to refrain from sex outside of marriage. However, given that the Episcopal denomination does not recognize same-sex marriages, it has created a no-win situation.

The 1979 resolution has never been entered into canon law, which means that its status is unclear. Whether or not it is binding on the bishops has been fiercely debated. Bishop Spong of New Jersey, for example, has ordained several gay men who are in long-term relationships. On the whole, though, most bishops have chosen to accept the authority of the General Convention on this matter. The issue of ordaining homosexuals is a controversial one, and sure to alienate people no matter what stance the church leadership takes. By accepting the 1979 resolution as law, many bishops have been able to claim that the matter is out of their hands. At least it keeps them from getting caught in the middle.

There is one group of Episcopalians who find the entire debate over ordaining homosexuals particularly perplexing. They are the many men who entered the priesthood not in spite of the fact that they were gay, but because of it. As these men are well aware, Episcopal bishops have been ordaining gay priests for decades.

Father Paul Wessinger wasn't sure whether the notices were supposed to be a joke or not. There were two of them, sitting on the dining room table at the seminary's refectory. One was on the healing of homosexuals. The other was on the healing of left-handed people.

Father Wessinger enjoyed his role as a spiritual director at Virginia Theological Seminary. Twice a month he would come up to Alexandria from his monastery and help young people explore their faith, help them learn how to open their minds and their hearts. Lately, though, he'd been noticing some rather hateful undertones to some of the seminary's policies. It seemed that the more open society got, the more closed the seminary became. The seminary was beginning to seem a little smug, and a little too sure of its stand: there can be no Christian expression of sexuality outside of marriage.

Eventually, Wessinger found a more detailed flyer tacked to one of the school's bulletin boards. Sure enough, someone was claiming to be able to cure homosexuality. Of all people, Father Wessinger knew how impossible that was. Homosexuality, like being left-handed, is something intrinsic to who you are. You may choose not to act on it, you may get married to cover it up, or you may even become a celibate monk. But that does not change the essence of what you are.

Three weeks later, Father Wessinger decided to say something about it in his monthly address to the seminary.

"I thank you for accepting me, for really knowing me as a spiritual director. It's been very, very important to me. It's been the culmination of my ministry. But a small voice in me is just saying, 'If they really knew about me, what would they think?'

"After I saw that notice in the refectory, the voice started screaming. I have to let you know that I am not a repentant homosexual, I am not a healed gay, I just happen to be a seventy-seven-year-old celibate monk who *is* gay.

"In the beginning, when I was a seminarian, I asked to be healed from it. And instead of being healed from it, I just became more and more compulsive. I had a lot of really dangerous and negative sexual experiences. And it didn't stop until I asked to be healed *as* a gay person."

Father Wessinger belongs to the Order of St. John the Evangelist, a small community of about twenty-two priest-brothers. The members of the community take vows of chastity, poverty, and obedience. Their mother house is in Cambridge, Massachusetts, and they have a separate retreat house just north of Boston. Until 1993, they also ran a third house in Durham, North Carolina.

Paul Wessinger entered the order in 1939, when he was twenty-four years old. Like many of his brothers at St. John's, he became a monk because he was terrified of his own sexuality.

"I arrived at it as my own decision. I think that—no, I'm sure that it was right, but I was terribly frightened. And because I entered at twenty-four, I never was in a committed relationship. That's affected my life in a lot of ways. Sometimes I was very angry at God, because God called me into a community before I'd had a committed relationship."

It took Paul a long time to work through his anger and regret. The events of the past few years, though, have done a lot to ease the bitterness. Now, at least, Paul and his brothers can talk openly about what they have given up for the order, and what they have gained from it.

In a perverse sort of way, the antigay rulings of the Episcopal General Convention have done much to liberalize certain bodies within the church. Paul, for example, had long suspected that most of his brothers at St. John's had joined the order for the same reason he had. The General Convention's resolutions gave them a catalyst to begin talking about the subject. Over a period of several years they were able to open up to each other, talking about their regrets, their fears, their secrets. This has made St. John's a much friendlier place of late. Physical contact has become less suspect; formal greetings have been replaced by warm hugs.

The community has also been looking for ways to make the church a more welcoming place for those gays who don't choose to join a monastery.

In 1991 and 1992 they hosted conferences on "The Journey of Gay Christians." And when a gay Roman Catholic group was evicted from its church in Durham, St. John's provided them with meeting space.

"We believe that it's important for us to be witnessing to celibacy," explains Father Wessinger, "but at the same time not to be witnessing to celibacy in conscious distinction to those gays and lesbians who are living in committed relationships."

The order demonstrated its support for such committed relationships in 1992. For several years, one of the brothers had, with the help of the bishop's wife, been running a married couples' retreat for Episcopal priests and their spouses. Being a member of the clergy can put unique strains on a marriage: priests, who are so accustomed to helping other couples work through their problems, often find it difficult to talk to anyone about their own. The brother was able to offer the priests the same sort of counsel that they provided their parishioners. He was a good listener, who could, in turn, get couples to truly listen to each other. Many of the couples who came back from the retreat had glowing things to say about the experience.

Several gay Episcopal priests who were living in long-term relationships heard about the retreats and how successful they were. They approached the brother and asked if he would consider holding one for them. The brother took the matter to his community and asked what they thought. Would this be moral?

It is difficult to describe exactly how St. John's handles controversial questions like this. The issue is eventually put to a vote, but the community seems to arrive at a consensus long before it is ever taken. "The head of the community put the whole thing right in front of us as to whether or not this retreat was right," says Father Wessinger. "We thought about it, discerned about it for six months. And nobody voted against it."

In the end, eight gay couples took part in the retreat as well as two of the brothers from St. John's. Being celibate monks, they weren't lovers, of course—at least not in the way that most people understand the term. One of the monks, Brother Thomas, said that before the retreat he had never understood why people wanted the church to bless gay relationships. Afterward, though, he could see how crucial it was.

After his coming out speech, Father Wessinger continued to serve as a spiritual director at Virginia Theological Seminary for another year, until St. John's closed its house in Durham and he returned to Cambridge. Many of the students had not agreed with what he'd said, but he was pleased to find that they did not reject him because of it. Until the day he left, he continued to have lively debates with several of the students on whether or not gays could be "healed." They never did come to an agreement, but it was heartening that they could still talk to each other.

Richard Bardusch finished divinity school in the spring of 1992. With no prospect of entering the priesthood, he went to West Virginia and spent the next year working as an advisor for a college dorm and thinking about his situation. Richard had never been particularly sexual. He dated infrequently, and he had never been in a long-term relationship with anyone. Still, the idea of one day falling in love and settling down is awfully hard to give up. But then so is a calling to the ministry.

In the spring of 1993, Richard came back to Durham and made an appointment to see Bishop Huntington Williams, who had taken over the ordination duties from Bishop Estill. Richard offered to take a vow of celibacy if he could begin the ordination process again. Bishop Williams agreed.

Since then several members of the clergy have intimated to Richard that the vow isn't all that binding. "Everyone expects you to take the vow," they say, "but no one's going to be checking up on you, understand?" This idea strikes Richard as very peculiar—that he could wind up entering the priesthood by making a vow that he wasn't expected to keep. Although he's not entirely happy with the bargain he's made, he intends to keep his end of it.

"I haven't given up on the Church," he says, "though I continue to struggle with all this. For me, it's sort of like selling a part of who I am for something else."

Richard's church in Durham, St. Philip's, has been very supportive of his new attempt to enter the priesthood. In his meetings with the Parish Discernment Committee, they have talked about how being gay will affect his ministry. Unlike the commission in 1990, however, they see his sexuality not as a problem but as an opportunity.

As Richard explains it, "Gay people are sensitized to what it means to be an outsider, part of the oppressed. That's very much an intrinsic part of the Christian message. The Christian message is for people who are downtrodden, who are oppressed, who are broken—whether in a social way, or in a psychological way, or in what you want to label a sinful way. What the Christian message does is offer hope and freedom and liberation. And we kind of screw that up sometimes in church. You know, in the Gospel of Luke, when Jesus began his ministry, the text he preached from was, 'I have come to bring liberation to the the captive, sight to the blind, freedom to the oppressed.' "

CHAPTER 5

The Long-Term Cost:
The Reverend Jim Lewis

Charleston, West Virginia, 1976. It was one of the few times that auditions for the musical *1776* had ever required police protection. The man trying out for the part of Thomas Jefferson was the Reverend Jim Lewis, the priest of St. John's Episcopal Church, and the police were there to make sure that nothing happened to him. A couple of weeks earlier they'd been warned that a group of fundamentalist Christians was planning to assassinate the priest or murder his children. Only a few years before, that sort of tip would have been treated as a crank call, too ludicrous for the police to take seriously. Now it seemed all too credible.

To Reverend Lewis it seemed as if the fight was never going to end. The musical was a much-needed diversion—a chance to meet new people and talk about something besides the ongoing battle over school textbooks. In truth, Lewis had never meant to get so deeply involved in that conflict. He had just been a concerned parent with four children in the public school system. It was hard to believe that things had gotten so out of hand.

In 1974 the Kanawha County School Board had adopted a new set of textbooks for its language arts courses. The books were some of the first multiethnic, multicultural texts to become available in the United States. They were designed to expose high school students to literature from cultures outside the Western European tradition. Much to the school board's surprise, the new textbooks ignited a firestorm of protest.

In a move that would foreshadow the political alliance of the 1980s, right-wing Republicans joined forces with fundamentalist Christians to condemn what they called the "mongrelization of America." As far as they were concerned, the United States had been established on the basis of a white, Christian, European heritage, and they were willing to fight to protect that. In the end, the struggle became more violent than anyone had thought possible. The school board building was bombed along with several high schools, and one fundamentalist preacher was convicted of conspiracy in the bombings.

Although the religious right never succeeded in controlling a majority of the school board through the electoral process, the intimidation tactics worked. The board backed down, officially leaving the decision on which textbooks to use in the hands of the individual school principals. Most principals, who were quite reasonably afraid for their schools and their families, chose not to adopt the new books. Later in the year, the school board adopted a request from the religious right on new restrictions for social studies classes. From now on, teachers were discouraged from being critical of U.S. actions, such as the treatment of Native Americans or the internment of Japanese Americans during World War II. Instead, they were required to teach that the United States is a country to be revered, with a moral and religious destiny to fulfill.

Reverend Lewis was one of those who spoke out in favor of the multicultural textbooks, and as a result he became a target of the fundamentalists. Not that Lewis minded a good fight, but this one seemed to go on forever, and he was getting tired. All that Jim Lewis wanted right then was a little peace and quiet.

He wasn't going to get it. Shortly after the final performance of *1776*, one of the other cast members dropped by Lewis's office in St. John's. He was a likable fellow, who wrote speeches for the governor and played guitar at his Roman Catholic church. After a few minutes of nervous talk, the man confessed that there was something important that he wanted to tell Lewis. The man hemmed and hawed for several more minutes, unsure how to bring up the subject. Finally he blurted it out. He was gay.

That was the first time that Reverend Lewis had ever heard such an admission from a friend. Lewis had been a marine, and before that a college athlete. He hadn't just laughed at the locker room jokes about fags, he'd told a few himself. But laughing at fags in the abstract is very different from actually knowing one.

"For about an hour, this man poured out his heart to me. He described his condition, the threat of loss of job if anyone at work would discover his gayness, his fear of being discovered in his church where he played a leadership role, and finally his frustration at not having any place to meet other homosexuals to talk about problems. All that seemed available at that time was a local gay bar."

Lewis didn't feel that he could do much about the man's fear or pain. But he could at least offer him a place to meet and talk. Under Lewis's leadership, St. John's had opened itself up as a community center, providing space for anyone who needed it. Alcoholics Anonymous, union organizers, a women's counseling center, a group of Vietnam veterans, and a youth soccer program all met there. In general, providing space for a group did not mean that the church necessarily endorsed its goals.

Still, Lewis figured he'd better get approval from the Vestry, the board of lay members who manage the day-to-day running of an Episcopal church. He spoke at one of their meetings, outlining why the homosexuals wanted to use the community center and why he thought they should be allowed to. As Lewis had expected, there were a number of people on the Vestry who were not pleased with the idea of homosexuals meeting on church property. The majority of the Vestry, however, felt that whether they agreed with Lewis on this one or not, they should leave him free to follow his own conscience. He was a good man, and they trusted him.

A few weeks later, the first small gathering of gay men and lesbians took place at St. John's. The group invited Reverend Lewis to attend, and he eagerly accepted. As he admits now, he was very curious about gay people. "Sex has always interested me. So when I met gay men and lesbians, I was curious. I wanted to know more about it. I wanted to know what they did, who they were. I was not offended, I was interested."

Over the next few months, the meetings grew to about thirty people, and Reverend Lewis kept attending.

"I learned so much in those months: things that I had either only read about or which I just had no real knowledge of at all. Many stereotypes I had about homosexuals were destroyed, and I came to have a real compassion for the trials and troubles these men and women faced."

While Lewis was learning about the gay community, it was learning about him as well. As word of the accepting priest spread, gay people from churches all over Charleston began seeking him out. Many of them had no one else to talk to. Of the first eight to contact him, six said they were planning to commit suicide. Lewis knew little about homosexuals, but he knew that as God's children their lives were precious gifts that should not be wasted. After speaking with him, all of the six chose to go on living.

Some people came to Lewis because they thought that he could make them straight. Lewis was not sure how to help them—after all, he had no idea what made people gay or straight in the first place. But he did try to support them in their attempts to change themselves. He even thought that one man might have succeeded.

Most of the people who approached him, though, were not looking for a way to change their sexuality. As Lewis put it, they came, "locked into the homosexual matrix, accepting their fate (though not understanding it) and in search of a way to live their homosexuality out in a responsible and even moral way." Of this group, there were two men who came to Lewis with a special request—they had been together for some time and wanted to have their relationship blessed in a church and recognized by their families. They wanted to be married.

"Both men were living together," wrote Lewis, "and wanted to deepen their commitment to each other by declaring their love toward each other and their intention to live faithfully, lovingly, and nonpromiscuously with each other. They were in search of God's legitimization of their love."[1]

Shortly thereafter, two women came to Lewis also asking to be married.

"I was totally unprepared for such a request," recalls Lewis. "There had been nothing in my theological training or in my present liturgical or theological frame of reference that would guide me. I felt very much on my own."

In one sense, it seemed to the priest that this was exactly the sort of business that the church was supposed to be in: witnessing covenants and encouraging monogamous relationships. But these were lesbian and gay relationships. What should his role be here?

He decided to begin by meeting with the couples, to find out why they wanted these blessings. After all, if it turned out that they weren't really serious, then he could stop the process and know that he was doing the right thing. But after several weeks of counseling them, he began to understand. They were, when all was said and done, looking for exactly the same things from their church that a heterosexual couple asked for when they got married: they wanted to say that this is a relationship that is going to last. They wanted to make a commitment in front of their friends, in front of their families, and in front of their God.

That still left the question, however, of whether it could ever be moral for Lewis to bless a homosexual relationship. In 1977, the Episcopal denomination had not yet taken any formal stand on homosexuality. So Lewis went back to the source—the Bible. What did it say about homosexuality and, more particularly, about loving, monogamous relationships between homosexuals? Surprisingly, he discovered that it had very little to say on the subject: "To begin with, I found that the simple injunction that 'The Bible prohibits such a union and sees homosexuality as a sin,' is simply not so. The Bible is silent about the love commitment of two homosexuals desiring a lasting and moral relationship with each other."

As Lewis found, the Bible doesn't talk about homosexuality that much, and when it does, the meaning is often ambiguous. The story of Sodom and Gomorrah, for example, is frequently cited as an example of God's condemnation of homosexuals. On a careful rereading, however, Lewis— like Jimmy Creech at Fairmont Methodist—decided that the story isn't actually about homosexuality at all: "Gerhard Von Rad in the now-classic commentary on *Genesis* points out that the real sin of Sodom is the sin of inhospitality to strangers. Entertaining angels unaware and refusing to see a message of God in a stranger was a constant stumbling block to the Hebrew people. Such a phenomenon continued into the New Testament as Jesus goes unrecognized and his disciples warned that a town that persecutes the messengers of God will have no more mercy shown to it that Sodom (Luke 10:1–12)."[2]

Lewis did find some very clear prohibitions in Leviticus. But he wasn't sure that it was fair to hold homosexuals to these Jewish purity codes, when Christians so routinely violated every other aspect of them. According to Leviticus, it is forbidden to eat pork or shellfish, or to collect interest on loans. As Lewis saw it, if we were to apply the rules of Leviticus evenly,

"None of us would come out of it justified. Death and judgment would belong to us all."

Last, Lewis consulted the letters of Paul, which forbid a wide variety of sexual activities. "Many people like to go to the Pauline epistles addressed to Rome and Corinth for ammunition to slay homosexuals. I can only say that as I study these passages I am not helped at all. The Greek words used by Paul are confusing in the Romans passage and open to various interpretations. It does appear to me that Paul may have been writing to guide the Church away from entering into the practice of temple prostitution and the worship of fertility gods through sexual manipulation. He does not seem to be addressing himself to people who are seeking loving relationships with other people of their own sex."[3]

None of this did much to resolve Reverend Lewis's problem. A clear biblical prohibition on the blessing would have let him say "no" with a clear conscience. But while the Bible didn't forbid such a blessing, it certainly wasn't endorsing it either. Left without a firm scriptural answer, Lewis spent several weeks grappling with his own basic sense of right and wrong.

In the midst of this struggle, he received a letter from a friend who was a priest in the hunt country of Virginia. He had written to tell Jim about a beautiful ceremony they performed in his parish every year around Thanksgiving time, in which they bless the hounds before the fall hunt. Blessing hounds? Lewis thought about that, and wondered why he had been struggling so hard with a question that suddenly seemed so simple.

"I have prayed over legislature, hot food at banquets, beauty contests, athletic events, prayer breakfasts, new homes, and dozens of other events. . . . I know some history which reminds me that the Church has blessed certain wars and even christened battleships and troops marching off to war."[4]

It occurred to Reverend Lewis that if he could bless an omelette, he could certainly bless two people's love.

When Lewis told Bishop Robert Atkinson about his plans for the ceremony, the bishop looked at him skeptically. Atkinson was not at all sure that this was a good idea. But the bishop believed that his priests should be free to follow their own consciences, and he had confidence in Lewis not to make any rash decisions. Lewis went ahead.

Although the blessings were called "liturgies of friendship," the ceremonies were nearly identical to those for a heterosexual wedding. Family and friends gathered in the church. The Eucharist was celebrated, prayers were said, and the couples exchanged their vows to love each other with God's help.

Reverend Lewis would have liked to announce the ceremonies publicly during Sunday services and invite the whole congregation, as he would have done for any other wedding. The couples, however, asked him not to. They wanted a small, quiet wedding, and if word got out a mob of reporters and protesters would turn the whole event into a sideshow. Reverend Lewis respected the couples' wishes. After the services were complete, he went to the Vestry and informed its members of what had taken place.

The Vestry was more than a little uneasy with the idea of having their priest blessing homosexual relationships. "Few of them would have done what I did if they'd been in my shoes," wrote Lewis after his meeting with them. "But they lovingly admitted that they were not in my shoes, and must respect the integrity of my decision."[5]

Lewis also suggested that now would be a good time to inform the rest of the congregation about the ceremonies. The Vestry, however, thought that the matter should be allowed to quietly go away. Publicizing it would just stir up trouble. The senior warden of the Vestry was Stanley Eastman, who worked for Union Carbide. As he put it to Jim, "At Carbide we have a saying: Wouldn't it be better if we washed this one downstream?"

"Well, we can wash this one downstream all right," answered Lewis, "but eventually someone is going to have to drink it."

In May of 1977, the Charleston *Daily Mail* ran an article reporting that Reverend Lewis had "married" two same-sex couples in St. John's Episcopal Church. The response was immediate.

"All hell broke loose when that became a public matter," remembers Lewis. "Some of the priests in the Episcopal church wanted to try me and have my priesthood taken away. And some people in my own church wanted to have me fired, to get rid of me."

Lewis had known that he was doing a dangerous thing. But he had never really understood just how much hatred and anger the idea of a gay or lesbian marriage could stir up. The more he tried to explain what he had done and why, the more furious people got. Strangers phoned him up to call him names—"fag," "queer," "cocksucker." His children were harassed in school. One night while Lewis was out, one of his children answered the phone.

"Do you know where your father is?"

"He's out."

"Do you know where he is?"

"No."

"He's out with fags at a gay bar." Click.

If anything, the harassment only expanded Lewis's sympathy for homosexuals, who had to put up with such treatment all the time. It had been one thing to hear their stories of persecution, quite another to experience it first hand. For the first time, Lewis felt he understood what it must be like to be gay, to live with fear and threats.

"I have discovered that homosexuals are modern day lepers," he wrote in a letter to his congregation. "Since I have associated myself with them I have been called 'queer' and my children have even taken abuse at school for my stand. I see Jesus touching lepers, associating himself with the oppressed and the outcasts. The gay question is a question of oppression for they are an oppressed people."[6]

Not everyone was opposed to what Lewis had done. But by and large, those who supported him were much quieter about their feelings than the people who wanted him tried for heresy. Lewis recalls that at the table one night, "one of my children said that a friend's mother had read the article in the *Daily Mail* and loved me for what I had done. She didn't understand what I had done, but she loved the way I seemed to stand up for the underdog."

Under the Episcopal system, the Vestry has the power to select a rector for the church or to request that the bishop dismiss him. The petition drive culminated in an open meeting at which every member of St. John's would have a chance to speak. The Vestry would then vote on Lewis's future as the rector of the church.

On Tuesday, the last day of May 1977, Reverend Lewis, Bishop Atkinson, the Vestry, and several hundred parishioners gathered for the meeting. Some of the church members were furious with Lewis and quoted Bible verses to condemn his actions. Others were supportive, arguing that Lewis had done good work for St. John's and should be allowed to follow his own conscience on this issue. For his part, Reverend Lewis agreed not to bless any more couples until the church as a whole had had a chance to "wrestle this issue through."

"The intensity of response to my simple service honoring the love between two people has been so tremendous that I have become fully aware that this is an area of deep emotion and fear for most of us. We need to look at that and deal with it, not sweep it under the rug or hide it in the closet."[7]

The defining moment came when members of the congregation began standing up and talking about their own hidden lives. Until that evening, the members of St. John's, like most people in 1977, firmly believed that they didn't actually know any homosexuals. And with good reason. Coming out publicly in 1977 Charleston was not a safe thing to do. Homosexuals hid their identities from even close friends and family. When the *Charleston Gazette* tried to interview members of the gay community about their reaction to the meeting, it was unable to find a single person who would let his or her name be used.[8]

Immediately following the meeting, the Vestry began its deliberations on the matter. At 1 A.M. on Wednesday morning, they emerged with their resolution. It was, quite simply, a statement "reaffirming the ministry of Jim Lewis as the Rector of St. John's."

Jim Lewis had a long and generally happy tenure at St. John's, where he remained until 1982. The Episcopal denomination did eventually address homosexual relationships, though not in the manner that Lewis would have liked. In 1979 the General Convention passed its resolution stating that homosexuality is incompatible with Christian teaching and forbidding any bishop from ordaining a practicing homosexual. Since that resolution, Lewis has presented three gay candidates for the priesthood, all of whom took a vow of celibacy.

In recent years, several attempts have been made to remove all mention of sexuality from the qualifications for the priesthood, which would put gay candidates on an equal footing with straight ones. At two recent General Conferences, such motions passed among the Episcopal clergy but were voted down by the lay members. Still, Reverend Lewis is hopeful that change will come.

"There is a lot of yeasty stuff going on. There are a number of laypeople and priests that are coming out of the closet in this church. I can't say that there are any bishops out of the closet. There are gay bishops, but they've been slow to come out."

Lewis knows that his stand on gay and lesbian issues has hurt his career in the Episcopal church. He's lost several postings to churches where he wanted to serve when the search committees found out about his involvement with the gay community. He remembers one particular case when he was being interviewed by a church in Memphis. Several members of the Vestry had taken him out to their country club, and wanted to speak to him about his résumé. For two hours they grilled him about the one line that read, "Worked with the gay and lesbian community." To Lewis, the whole situation seemed ridiculous. Finally, he asked them, "Why are you spending so much time on one line of my résumé, when there are so many causes I've been involved with? Why don't you ask about my involvement with racial concerns and how I feel about being interviewed in a segregated country club?"

Not surprisingly, Lewis didn't get the job. He's philosophical about it. "Sure, it's cost me," he admits. "I'm marked forever. It's affected my career. But this isn't supposed to be a *career*, anyway."

Reverend Lewis eventually came to work for Bishop Estill in Raleigh, as the diocese's director of social ministries. The bishop gave Lewis a free hand to work on a wide variety of social issues, from the problems of AIDS and drug abuse to the plight of migrant farm workers to initiatives for world peace. It was during this time that Lewis met Nancy Kepple, helped keep Willie Pilkington out of jail, participated in the Raleigh hearings on nondiscrimination, and became a founding member of the Raleigh Religious Network for Gay and Lesbian Equality.

In 1994 Lewis, a bit older and wiser, was once again approached by a lesbian couple seeking marriage. As he had almost twenty years before, he met with the couple to determine their sincerity, and as before, he found himself agreeing to perform the ceremony. After consulting with family, the couple decided on May 14 as the date for the ceremony—the same day on which the diocese would be installing a new bishop. Shortly after the news of the ceremony Lewis intended to perform became public, Bishop Estill issued a "Godly Admonition" to every priest in the diocese, warning them that performing such a ceremony "would constitute a deliberate and specific violation of one's ordination vows." Lewis was also informed that he would be fired as soon as the new bishop took office.

Lewis initially planned to go ahead with the wedding anyway. After all, this wasn't the first job he'd lost over his stand on gay and lesbian issues. Yet a Godly Admonition is a serious matter in the Episcopal church. For disobeying it, Lewis would be put on trial in ecclesiastical court and would probably be stripped of his priesthood. Under that threat, Lewis finally backed down. "I feel like a hypocrite," he admitted, "like I'm abandoning them."

The couple went ahead with their wedding ceremony nevertheless. Although both the women were Episcopalian, no Episcopal priest would risk performing the ceremony, and they were forced to use a minister from another denomination.

As for Lewis, he is still looking forward to the day when the Church embraces its gay and lesbian members.

"What people felt when I came to Charleston in 1974 was that an old way of life was dying. I'm interested in seeing the Church preside over the birth of something new, rather than being the coroner for something old."

CHAPTER 6

A Place to Meet: St. John's Metropolitan Community Church

Florida, 1966. June Norris was a devout Seventh-Day Adventist and believed in the sanctity of marriage. Still, in 1966 she decided that enough was enough and divorced the man to whom she'd been married since she was fifteen years old. Because she had never finished high school, June decided to take the equivalency test. By the end that year she had passed the GED, and two things had become clear to her. First, her former husband would never leave her alone while they were both living in the same state. Second, since Florida had no junior college system, she wouldn't be able to afford to continue her education if she stayed where she was. So that fall she packed up everything she owned and drove west to Los Angeles.

June had a number of relatives living in Los Angeles, including a sister. But between schoolwork and church work and the necessity of earning a living, she didn't have much time to spend with them. She went to East Los Angeles College at night and worked days at White Memorial, a Seventh-Day Adventist hospital. Somehow she did manage to make time for her nephew, Ted Sweet. In spite of the difference in age and background the two of them had hit it off. They were never at a loss for things to talk about, and they became fast friends.

In 1970 Ted told June that he was gay. "I thought he meant that he was happy," remembers June. "I had never heard the term. Seventh-Day Adventists are pretty sheltered, and I had spent twenty-nine years in a *very* sheltered marriage. When I finally left that marriage, I had tried to get in touch with what the world was like, but not anything outside my beliefs or my religion."

Seeing that June didn't understand what he was saying, Ted explained it more precisely. After several tries, June finally got it. It was not something that she was at all prepared to deal with. She smiled politely, trying not to let Ted see how horrified she was. Fortunately Ted had to leave a few minutes later, and June didn't have to keep up the charade for long.

June prided herself on being a rational person. As soon as Ted left, she went down to the public library to learn everything she could about homosexuality. All that she could find, though, were Sigmund Freud's theories about absent or ineffectual father figures. That didn't have much to do with Ted's situation, and it certainly wasn't of any practical use to her in figuring out how she should behave around him. So she sat down and tried to reason it out for herself.

"There was no way I would want to destroy the confidence that he had in me, the way he had shared himself. The fact that he had shared who he really was with me shouldn't make any difference in our relationship, because he hadn't changed. The only thing that had changed was that I had certain information that I didn't have prior to that day."

June resolved not to let this new information ruin her relationship with Ted. She buried her own discomfort with the subject and allowed him to open his life to her. She listened to Ted talk about his lover, and she met some of his gay friends. Slowly she got over the shock. These were decent, intelligent, and fun people. She could see why Ted enjoyed being around them. Ted's lover, Lee, was a friendly young minister, and it was hard to dislike him. More than that, Lee and Ted really seemed to care about each other. One day June found herself offering Ted advice on how to deal with a rough spot in his relationship. That was when she realized how thoroughly she had come to accept it.

Lee was a minister at the Metropolitan Community Church (MCC), a new church that had been created to serve homosexuals who felt unwelcome in the denominations in which they had been raised. Lee and Ted had been trying to get June to come to a service for months, but she kept making excuses. June could accept that Ted was gay, and she could accept his relationship with Lee. But the idea of a gay church seemed preposterous.

Lee had a good singing voice, and one Saturday June invited him to come and sing at her Seventh-Day Adventist church. Afterward, Lee and Ted finally convinced her to at least go by and see the new building that MCC was about to move into. It was an old building that the church had just purchased, and the congregation was in the process of renovating it. June still remembers seeing the new church for the first time.

"As I approached the building, the first thing I noticed was that beautiful stained-glass window. It was Jesus with his arms outstretched as if he were saying, 'Come unto me.' And I thought, 'Ooh. This is a *real* church.' I guess I wasn't prepared for that. Because when we stepped inside, there was this presence. It was a feeling of love, of holiness. And as I was standing on the balcony, looking down at the people who were working so hard to prepare the church for its worship service the next day, and the choir practicing in the corner, I heard God speak to my heart. It was like I heard the words, but I didn't hear them with my ears. And the words were, 'This is my house.'

"And I knew that God had told me that it was OK to be gay and Christian. I knew that I was somehow going to be connected with this church."

June was working six days a week at the hospital, so it wasn't until that fall that she had a Sunday free to go to a service. She immediately felt right at home. After several visits, she enrolled in a membership class and began doing volunteer work for MCC's crisis intervention center.

In the early 1970s, there were very few places for gays in trouble to turn. MCC ran one of the first helplines for gay callers, and kept some extra beds in the church for people with noplace else to go. For homosexuals thinking about suicide or gay teenagers who'd been thrown out by their parents, MCC was a place of comfort and aid. June's involvement with the crisis intervention center lasted several months, and she counseled hundreds of callers. Her initial naiveté, however, caused more than a few chuckles among the other volunteers.

During the crisis center training program, one meeting was devoted to recognizing various drugs and their effects. Larry Long, the instructor for the class, began with marijuana, saying, "I'm sure we can all recognize this one, so there's no need to go into it."

June raised her hand at this point and interrupted. "I'm sorry, but I don't know how to recognize marijuana; is that a white powder?"

Larry groaned and covered his face to conceal his smile. "OK, we'll cover marijuana."

Through her work on the helpline, June quickly made a number of good friends at MCC. As word got out about her, she found herself making even more. As a straight woman in a gay denomination, June was in a unique position. A number of people in the congregation asked if she would speak to their parents, to help them understand. June found herself meeting with worried families, listening to concerned mothers, talking with anxious fathers. From her time on the helpline, she had begun to understand how hard life could be for children who realized they were gay. Now she was beginning to understand how hard it was for their parents as well.

That fall, as she was taking an MCC course analyzing the Bible's statements about sexuality, June felt a strong and sudden calling, an absolute conviction about what she was supposed to be doing with her life. She went to the Reverend Troy Perry, the founder of MCC, and told him that she wanted to continue her studies and work toward becoming a minister. "He just hugged me," she says, "and said he'd been wondering how long it would take before I knew that.

"I recognized that a big part of my ministry was going to be to help people accept themselves. I had heard the stories of how difficult it was to be a gay teenager, to recognize that he or she was different, and how they felt led to suicide so many times. And how the church itself was the oppressor. They believed, if they had been brought up in a church-going environment, that somehow they were obnoxious to God. And they had a hard time believing that God loved them just the way they were. And I can't tell you the joy that comes from knowing that someone finally believes it, to see that discovery in their faces and their lives, how lives were turned around and people changed by the power of God in their lives. It was a very wonderful and fulfilling ministry."

That ministry was not without its costs, however. June had talked about her new church with several of her co-workers at White Memorial, and word had reached her boss. He called her into his office and informed her that while he appreciated her empathy for those in trouble, she was not to bring homosexual gossip to work. He then handed her a letter stating that White Memorial Hospital did not approve of her discussing homosexuality in any way, shape, or form. June was required to sign the letter to acknowledge that she had read it, and it was placed in her permanent work record. June was then demoted from her position as a supervisor.

As things worked out, the demotion didn't last long. A year later, White Memorial needed a new supervisor for the outpatient business office. The business manager had heard what an efficient supervisor June had been in her previous department, and he didn't particularly care what she talked about with the staff during coffee breaks as long as she got the job done. He offered her the position, and June accepted.

Not everything could be undone so easily. By the end of 1972 June was attending Samaritan, MCC's seminary in Los Angeles. Between her job at the hospital, her seminary studies, and her volunteer work for the helpline, June was spreading herself thin. Eventually Troy Perry stepped in and told her point blank to take a break from the crisis intervention center before she collapsed. That's why June wasn't in the church building that night in January of 1973.

Her nephew, Ted, was working the helpline alone that night. He had made the rounds of the church, making sure that everything was locked up and the lights were out, and had just gotten back to the crisis center. He noticed that all the lights on the phone had lit up at once, but it wasn't ringing. Then all the lights on the phone went out, and when he picked it up, it was dead.

Downstairs, someone started pounding on the door and screaming. The church was located in a fairly rough neighborhood, which made Ted somewhat reluctant to open the door in the middle of the night. But the pounding and the shouting were so insistent that he had to find out what the problem was. When he opened the door, he found a man shouting in Spanish and pointing at the roof.

Ted had no idea what the man was shouting about, but eventually he looked up to see what he was pointing at. Horrified, he saw flames coming up through the roof of the church. Knowing the phones in the church were dead, Ted tried to tell the man to run home and phone the fire department. But because Ted spoke no Spanish and the man spoke no English, they didn't make much headway. A crowd gathered to watch the fire, and eventually someone arrived who was bilingual. Ted's request was relayed, and one of the neighbors made the call.

The church was completely destroyed. The arson investigation team labeled the fire "of suspicious origin" and hypothesized that someone had thrown flaming torches in through a window. Rumors and accusations floated around that someone had "burned the church for Jesus," but nothing was ever proved.

Although MCC was able to collect on its insurance policy, the congregation was unable to rebuild on the same location. The zoning laws had changed since the building had been constructed, and there was no space now available to build the parking lot required to meet them. The congregation struggled for several months, moving every few weeks, renting space in theaters. (To everybody's amusement, one of them still had signs up for the show *Queen for a Day*.) Eventually they bought an old domed opera house.

June was heartbroken. The new building looked nothing like the beautiful church with the stained-glass window that she had fallen in love with. Still, the congregation had a place to be together.

That year, at the denomination's general conference, June was licensed as an MCC pastor. She was the second woman to be ordained in the denomination, and the first heterosexual.

Wake Forest, North Carolina, 1975. In the South, the Baptist faith is still largely segregated by race. Like most black Baptists, Willie White had been raised in the National Baptist Convention. He was ordained at the age of eighteen at his little home church in East Texas. He'd gone on to attend Bailey University, a Southern Baptist College, and was now completing his studies at Southeastern Baptist Seminary in Wake Forest. He was also beginning to tell people about his sexuality.

Nineteen seventy-five was an interesting time to come out of the closet.

The gay rights movement was gaining momentum and had not yet encountered the fundamentalist backlash that would strike in the 1980s. When Willie told his friends in the seminary that he was gay, most of them were a bit surprised, but not particularly upset. No one implied that being gay made him a bad minister, and not one of them quoted a Bible verse in condemnation of homosexuality. At the time, it seemed as unreasonable as quoting the old biblical justifications for enslaving blacks.

During a trip to Washington, D.C., that year, Willie attended a service at an MCC church. He liked what he saw. The worship service was similar to that of most mainline Protestant denominations. They celebrated communion, and they recited the Apostles' and Nicene creeds. The principal difference was that MCC celebrated holy unions for same-sex couples.

To Reverend White, the idea of a denomination for gay men and lesbians made a lot of sense. Christianity was a religion for the outcast, the downtrodden. It seemed to him that homosexuals were exactly the people who needed Christ's message.

The next year, in 1976, Willie decided to start a gay Bible study class. He didn't know many gay people in the Wake Forest area, and he had no idea whether anyone would even turn up for such a class. There was only one way to find out. Willie drove out to the gay bars in Raleigh and Durham and put up signs announcing a Bible study group that would be meeting in his apartment.

Los Angeles, 1976. Some of June's gay friends thought that she was getting a bit reckless. She didn't seem to understand that the world could be a dangerous place for gay people—and for those who associated with them too openly. Her license plate read "JUN MCC." She lived alone, and her church work and her hospital work had her coming and going at all hours of the night. Even after the firebombing of the church, June never thought that anything could happen to her.

In 1976 the woman who lived next door to June was raped and murdered. Much to the relief of her friends, June decided that she simply couldn't live in that building anymore. Two of her friends, Tony and Wayne, persuaded her to share an apartment with them, and the three of them moved in together.

By coincidence, Tony began using the outpatient services at White Memorial. One day, when he came in for his doctor's appointment, he brought

June her watch, which she had left at home that morning. He was still there chatting with her when the new business manager came down to see June, so June introduced Tony, saying that he was her roommate.

Thirty minutes later, the business manager called June into his office. He informed her that she was fired from her job for being a poor moral example by living with a man to whom she was not married.

"Wait just a minute," June responded, "I'm living with *two* men that I'm not married to. And they're a couple, and everybody knows that there is nothing going on, that I am not being 'immoral' in your words."

The business manager stated that this was an even bigger outrage, and dismissed her. She appealed the decision all the way up the line, but to no avail. By April 1976, June was without a job.

Raleigh, North Carolina. As 1976 wore on, Reverend White's gay Bible study classes drew more and more people. After a few months, it was clear to Willie that it was time for the classes to grow into something more. He wrote to MCC's denominational headquarters in Los Angeles and asked for permission to form an MCC "study group"—the first step in creating a new congregation. The reply came back quickly; the request was approved.

At the time Reverend White was also serving as the pastor of a Baptist church in Henderson, North Carolina. It was a small rural church that only met for services twice a month. Willie knew that running two churches, even two small ones, would be more than he could handle. When he offered his resignation to the church in Henderson, he explained exactly why he was leaving and what he would be doing. The congregation was somewhat surprised to learn that their minister would be leaving to start a gay church, but showed no signs of being particularly upset by the fact. They did, however, ask him to continue as their pastor for another ninety days, to give the church time to find a replacement.

Los Angeles, 1977. June Norris wanted to fight her dismissal from White Memorial. "How can they fire me for who I choose to live with?" she wondered. "That's my business, not theirs." The ACLU, however, did not believe that she had a case. In their opinion, White Memorial was a private Seventh-Day Adventist hospital, and therefore could set whatever moral code of conduct for its employees that it chose to. June felt that the ACLU was missing the point. White Memorial received a great deal of money from Medicare and Medicaid, and as a recipient of government funds should be required to be an equal opportunity employer.

The whole thing seemed absurd. They weren't firing her for anything that she'd done on the job: they were firing her for who her roommates were. But without outside assistance, June couldn't afford to fight a legal battle. She started a small business of her own, doing taxes and bookkeeping.

Raleigh, 1977. By the end of 1976, Reverend White's MCC study group had outgrown his living room. The group was getting larger and had started to develop a sense of itself as a congregation. They had even chosen a name for their church, a church without a building—St. John's Metropolitan Community Church.

Reverend White began looking for a space to hold services, and he approached a Quaker meeting in Raleigh. As it turned out, the meeting house's schedule was being administered by Sister Evelyn Matron, a Roman Catholic nun.[1] Reverend White explained the situation to her and found a sympathetic ear. Since the Society of Friends can be notoriously slow in deciding controversial matters (as they themselves put it, Quakers are about making *right* decisions, not quick ones), Sister Evelyn gave St. John's permission to use the building until the meeting had fully considered the matter. St. John's held services in the meeting house for several weeks, until the Friends' meeting announced its decision—it did not want St. John's using the facility. Once again St. John's was looking for a home.

One of the members of St. John's was a professor at North Carolina State and happened to know Clay Stalnaker, a faculty member in the Division of Multi-disciplinary Studies. Clay had taught courses in philosophy and religion, and he was in touch with most of the churches in Raleigh through North Carolina State's Cooperative Campus Ministry. He seemed a logical person to ask for help.

The professor from St. John's visited Stalnaker in his office one afternoon. He told Clay that he and a group of other gays had been meeting in one another's homes for informal worship services. He explained how inconvenient the arrangement was—the spaces were always too small and the church could never advertise its location in advance. He asked if Clay could help them find a more permanent home, perhaps a church that would loan the space on Sunday afternoons or evenings, when the building would normally be empty. Stalnaker, for his part, had not even realized that his colleague was gay before this conversation. It took Clay a few seconds to get over his surprise. Then he said yes, he would be happy to help any group of Christians find a place to worship.

Stalnaker didn't think the task would be too difficult. He immediately thought of Pullen Baptist, and gave its pastor, Bill Finlater, a call. Clay was sure that Pullen, with its liberal record, would be happy to help out a minority group that wanted a place to meet and hold services. He was genuinely surprised when Reverend Finlater called him back a few days later to say that the Board of Deacons had decided that hosting the group would probably cause trouble.

Next Stalnaker approached the Unitarian Universalist church in Raleigh. Again he was almost sure that this church would agree to host St. John's. The Unitarian denomination was a staunch supporter of gay rights and had made public statements welcoming gays and lesbians as full members of the church. Here, however, St. John's met with the opposite problem. The Unitarians could well understand why homosexuals wouldn't want to attend a church that condemned them. But the Unitarian church didn't. Why did they need a separate homosexual church, when they could all be welcomed as members of the Unitarian church? In the end, they too turned down St. John's request for meeting space.

Stalnaker, by now a bit frustrated, next turned to the Reverend Steve Shoemaker, the Presbyterian campus minister. Stalnaker explained the situation to Shoemaker, and Steve agreed that the new group at least deserved a place to meet. The Presbyterian campus ministry controlled a student lounge in West Raleigh Presbyterian Church, and Reverend Shoemaker agreed to let St. John's use that for its worship services. But after the group had met there for two weeks, word leaked out to the congregation of West Raleigh. Shoemaker was confronted by the Session, the committee of lay members who run a Presbyterian church. They informed him that while he might control the lounge, they controlled the building. Having homosexuals meet on the grounds was deemed to be bad for the image of the church. St. John's was no longer welcome to use the space.[2]

Finally, Clay suggested that Willie try the Community United Church of Christ (CUCC). Like Pullen, it was a church with a reputation for liberal thinking. Most of its members had been raised in other denominations but had been drawn to CUCC by its work in the community and its willingness to deal with difficult social issues. Long before North Carolina's public schools had been integrated, CUCC had been working to promote racial understanding and social justice. In a particularly controversial move, the church had integrated its summer Bible school camp with those of local black churches. The idea of black and white children playing and studying the Bible together had been too much for some people, and the segregationists had gone wild. The local ABC affiliate's political commentator, Jesse Helms, conducted an almost nightly diatribe against the Community United Church of Christ and its vile intention to mix the races that God had clearly separated. Crosses were even burned in front of the church. But CUCC had gone ahead with its integrated summer camp. Clay figured that this was not a church that was likely to worry about what other people might think.

Trouble was, CUCC was currently without a minister, and Clay didn't know if its members were in a position to make a controversial decision like this. The new pastor, Cally Rodgers-Witte, had been called, but wasn't due to arrive for several months. Nevertheless, when Clay talked with a few members of the Church Council, they said that they would be willing to listen to any reasonable request.

On Sunday, March 27, Reverend White spoke at a meeting of CUCC's Church Council. He talked about the history of St. John's and of the Metropolitan Community Church, and why he felt that what they were doing was so important. He asked the council to let St. John's use CUCC's building for a 3 P.M. Sunday worship service.

The debate on the matter was rather sedate. "After all," one council member said, "it's not like we're turning the sanctuary into a gay bar. What's the big deal? A few men, gathered around a piano, singing hymns on Sunday."

A couple of council members did ask why gays felt the need for a separate church. Why not just join CUCC? "The answer," said Carolyn King, who was on the council at the time, "was that *they* felt the need for this fellowship, this support from each other." In the end a motion was made to allow the church as a whole to vote on the matter at the next congregational meeting, and it passed 8–5. According to one member of the council, St. John's request was discussed and voted on within fifteen minutes. The remaining hour and a half of the meeting was spent arguing about what to do with a shed that needed renovating.

The congregational meeting on April 17 was a bit livelier. Of the fifty-one members present, only one spoke out directly against St. John's request. A lot of people, though, had questions. Some asked what the effect would be on their children. Other parents responded that since their children were likely to find out about homosexuality sooner or later, they wanted that education to take place in the church, where they could discuss it with them. Carolyn King remembers, "The general response was, 'Well, church is where that should happen, in the context of Christian fellowship.' "

Other people worried that someone might burn down the church if word got out that homosexuals were meeting there. Some said that they just couldn't understand the whole gay lifestyle. One woman said that she thought St. John's holy unions were blasphemous. But there were other members who thought that the holy unions were the best service that St. John's offered for its members. How could they condemn anybody for wanting to live in committed, monogamous relationships?

In the end the argument that prevailed was the simple belief that everyone should have a place to worship. No matter how individuals felt about gays or gay rights, almost all of them believed that people should be able to get together and pray if they wanted to. The measure to provide space for St. John's worship services passed with twenty-six for and nine against.

St. John's began meeting at CUCC the next week. Now that it had a permanent home and could advertise its location, attendance quickly shot up from about ten or fifteen people a week to an average of thirty-five. That still filled only the first three pews on one side of the sanctuary, but it was enough to begin feeling like a community. For many gays, it was their first chance to be open in their church life, to appreciate all the things that their straight friends took for granted: going to church with your loved one, celebrating your relationship in the eyes of your God and your community, and knowing that the same community will be there for you when the time finally comes to mourn him or her.

Aside from the sight of grown men holding hands, St. John's services were much like those at any other church. "Very seldom did the church service deal with homosexuality," recalls Reverend White. "Being a gay

Christian is more than being gay. The Bible's spiritual development is far larger than the two or three passages on homosexuality."

In 1978 St. John's applied to become a member of the Cooperative Campus Ministry at North Carolina State. The campus ministers from the other denominations debated the matter for quite some time, and finally decided to approve the request. Willie White became MCC's campus minister. He established a student group, after the fashion of the Baptist Student Union and the Methodist Student Union. It was the first group for gay and lesbian students ever formed at the school.

As the years went by, that student group would eventually become completely secular, dropping St. John's from its name and becoming simply the Gay and Lesbian Student Union.

The Reverend Rufus Stark, then the pastor of Fairmont Methodist Church, did not find out about St. John's campus ministry for nearly a year. When he did, he was not at all pleased. What had the Cooperative Campus Ministry been thinking, letting in a bunch of homosexuals to pervert the word of God and corrupt impressionable young students? Stark wrote a series of letters to the members of the Cooperative Campus Ministry, demanding that they reconsider their decision and expel St. John's from their organization. After a very short debate, the Cooperative Campus Ministry wrote a letter back to Reverend Stark, informing him that they had sufficiently considered the matter the first time around.

Stark took his campaign to the press. In a letter to the *News and Observer,* he argued that St. John's campus ministry was a corrupting influence because it insisted that homosexuality was normal. How could anyone be permitted to expose college students to such a dangerous idea? "The homosexual condition is abnormal," argued Stark, "and treatable." Rather than trying to change society, gays should get the medical help that they so desperately need. He signed the letter "Reverend Rufus Stark, Fairmont United Methodist Church."[3]

Ten years later, another pastor of Fairmont would be severely chastised for using Fairmont's name when signing a letter based on his own opinions. Members of the congregation would argue that he had no right to speak out on gay and lesbian issues, if in doing so he appeared to represent their church. No one, however, complained to Rufus Stark when he stated his own position on homosexuality in 1979 and signed the church's name.

Los Angeles, 1980. June had been getting job offers for some time. New MCC churches were sprouting up faster than the denomination could train ministers. As an ordained MCC minister, June was constantly receiving letters from new churches that wanted her to come out for a visit and an interview. But June had always told them that she was happy being on staff at the mother church in Los Angeles. She liked her roommates, her business was doing well, and her daughter Dixie had moved to Los Angeles just a couple of years earlier. After a few years of her polite rejections, word got around that June wasn't interested, and the offers stopped coming.

All this made it even harder for June's friends to understand her behavior in 1979. She began telling her clients that she would be closing down her accounting business after the April 1980 tax season, and she told her roommates, Wayne and Tony, that they should start looking for a replacement for her. When they asked where she was going, June said that she didn't know. "I just felt very strongly that God was calling me out of Los Angeles, and I had no idea where."

June's friends and family were less than pleased with this explanation. Reasonable people, they argued, do not shut down their businesses because they think that God might be calling them somewhere when they don't even know where that somewhere might be. They pointed out that Tony and Wayne needed her help to meet the rent, and that Dixie had moved all the way out to Los Angeles to be with her. June's mother was also living in Los Angeles, having moved in with Ted and his new lover Bill. June's mother was eighty-nine years old and suffering from congestive heart failure. All of this suggested that now was a bad time for June to be leaving the city. None of it, however, changed the fact that June was sure she was going.

In November June got a call from the Reverend Nancy Radcliffe, the pastor of an MCC church in Columbia, South Carolina. June had met Nancy and her lover, Keri, at one of MCC's national conferences, and the three had become good friends and had kept in touch. Nancy had called to tell June about a little church in Fayetteville, North Carolina, that needed a pastor. She had been looking all over for a "June Norris type" to fill the position, and had finally decided to call and ask the real McCoy. June admitted that she was planning on leaving Los Angeles soon, although she didn't know where she would be going.

Word that June was leaving the mother church must have leaked out, because offers from other new churches flooded in over the next few months. In the end, it was the little church in Fayetteville that June decided on. In May of 1980 she packed up her car and left Los Angeles. Having never seen the new church, having never even been to Fayetteville, she began the long drive east to North Carolina.

Fayetteville, North Carolina, 1981. MCC Fayetteville was a much smaller church than June had imagined. The average attendance for Sunday worship was only ten people. After a few weeks of June's sermons, though, attendance rose to nearly thirty people a week. Still, June could tell that this group wasn't developing into a church.

"It was just a struggling little group. And I finally concluded that only a few of the people really wanted the church to be a church. A lot of them seemed to just want social activities, another way of contacting gay and lesbian people. There were some people who were really serious, but many just wanted it to be a social thing. It just wasn't developing into the church that it should have."

By 1981 St. John's had grown into a solid congregation. The Metropolitan Community Church had recognized it as a "mission stage" church, and its collection was running high enough that St. John's could afford to pay CUCC a small rent for the use of the property.

The relationship between St. John's and CUCC was working out quite well, although the two congregations didn't see that much of each other. It helped that the members of St. John's went out of their way to help with the yard work and with keeping the facilities clean. The Reverend Cally Rodgers-Witte says of her church's tenants: "St. John's has bent over backward to be careful—has been much better about taking care of the building than we have. You know that if you come in the next morning and the lights are still on and the windows and doors are unlocked or something, that it was our meeting and not theirs."

There was even one point when CUCC's choir was getting a bit thin, and they asked to borrow a few singers from St. John's. It turned out that CUCC's choir director was also a member of St. John's, so there was no problem getting volunteers.

All in all, the relationship with CUCC was running smoothly, and St. John's itself was stable. Reverend White recalls, "I had basically concluded that I had carried the church as far as I could carry it, and that it would be good for me and the church to have a change."

Willie and his lover, Robert Pace, left Raleigh at the end of 1981. They moved to New York, where Willie eventually became an MCC district coordinator (essentially, that denomination's equivalent of a bishop). In 1988, when Willie's parents died, the couple moved back to Houston, and now live eight blocks from the house where Willie grew up. As of the writing of this book, they have been together twenty years.

In the spring of 1981, at MCC's Gulf and Lower Atlantic District (GLAD) Conference, someone had the good sense to point out that the denomination now had two churches in North Carolina, one of which had a minister but couldn't afford to support her, the other of which had the resources to support a minister but didn't have one. A compromise was worked out whereby June Norris would split her time between the two churches. She would preach alternating Sundays at St. John's and MCC Fayetteville, and would arrange for a lay member of each church to deliver a sermon when she wasn't there.

June's sermons were popular, and over the course of that summer St. John's attendance increased to sixty people a week. MCC Fayetteville's continued to hang around thirty. By September June had decided that she simply couldn't make a go of the church in Fayetteville. She spoke with the district coordinator, who sent a student clergyperson to handle the ministry of MCC Fayetteville. June then informed St. John's that she would be available for them full time if they wanted her. The congregation elected her pastor effective October 1, 1981.

The first years went smoothly for June. Church attendance continued rising to about ninety a week, and the sanctuary wasn't looking so empty anymore. There were a few rumblings of discontent every now and then. June's basic message was that it's OK to be gay and that God loves you just the way you are. But some of the members felt that it was time to move beyond that message and to start talking about other things. Wayne Lindsey, who was a member at the time, says the feeling was, "OK, I came to church, and I was in a hurting place, and I needed to hear that message. But I've been here for six years. Now what?"

There were also a few troubles from outside the church. A number of men left threatening messages for June on St. John's answering machine. They assumed that as the pastor of a gay church, she must be a lesbian. Various voices suggested that she should "look over her shoulder" and described in detail the sexual acts they would perform on her when they caught her. This, they assured her, would make her see what she was missing with men.

On one occasion, a man who identified himself as a member of the Ku Klux Klan left a message saying that he intended to kill a bunch of queers, and if they didn't believe him, just wait until services tomorrow. June promptly called the police, who listened to the tape and then searched the building for bombs. The next morning, under police protection, worship services went on as planned. Although Reverend Rodgers-Witte was on sabbatical, the acting pastor of CUCC and his wife made a point of attending worship services with St. John's that afternoon. No violence occurred.

St. John's thus faced various problems in the early 1980s, but they all seemed beatable. If the members were willing to stand up and fight hard enough, it seemed they could overcome anything. By and large, the early 1980s were remembered as happy times by all involved, particularly given the wave of death that was about to hit.

"I guess the first person we really ministered to was Jerry Norris,"[4] says June. "He was very, very ill with AIDS, and had no place to go when they released him from prison. A person in the Wake County Health Department called me and asked if there was some way we could help. She said that he is not gay, but he doesn't have anybody. His family deserted him when he went into prison."

Social Services agreed to pay the rent on a house for Jerry, and St. John's decorated and furnished it for him. Members of the church signed on as his AIDS buddies, and helped him with the necessities of life—including having someone around to talk to.

Unfortunately, no one had told Jerry that all of this help was coming from a gay church. The people who had volunteered to work with him assumed that Jerry knew what the Metropolitan Community Church was all about. It never occurred to any of Jerry's AIDS buddies that they needed to come out to him, and it took Jerry several weeks to piece together the odd bits of double-entendre that had been confusing him.

"When he discovered that he was being surrounded by a bunch of lesbian and gay people," says June, "his macho image came to the forefront, and he didn't want any of them around him. So we stayed away for a little while. Finally, he called and said that he was sorry, that we were the ones who had befriended him, and that he was changing his attitude. He realized that he was totally alone without us."

Jerry's health declined rapidly, and he couldn't leave the house much. June remembers one of his last public outings, to St. John's annual Thanksgiving dinner. "We held hands and formed a circle to ask the blessing of the food. And I invited anybody to talk about what they were thankful for. And Jerry, standing there with two hands joined to two gay men, said that he was happier than he had ever been in his life. For the first time in his life he had a home and people who cared for him." Jerry died less than a month later, in December of 1985.

By the time Jerry was buried, June was ministering to five other people with AIDS, spread out across the state. Allen, for example, had once been a member of St. John's, but had recently moved back to Winston-Salem to be near his family. His mother was terrified of him. She made Allen eat off paper plates and drink out of disposable cups whenever he came to visit. But his brother and his friends stood by him. When the ambulance paramedics found that Allen had AIDS and refused to touch him, it was his brother who picked him up in his arms and drove him to the hospital. June made a two-hundred-mile trip every week to be able to spend time with Allen and give him communion. Each week she brought an old friend from St. John's to say hello and see how he was doing.

Allen died not long after Jerry. When planning the funeral service in Winston-Salem, Allen's mother made June promise not to mention what had killed her son or how he'd gotten it. She still hadn't told her new husband that Allen was gay or that he'd died of AIDS, and she didn't intend for him to find out now. June complied with the mother's wishes. But Allen's friends held a separate memorial service for him at St. John's, where they could recognize Allen for who he'd really been and mourn what had really happened to him.

A hundred miles in the opposite direction, June was ministering to David Huggins in Fayetteville. David had been a Bible teacher at St. John's. "I attended all his Bible studies, because he was just wonderful," remembers June. "He made a game out of it. It was good to see him use his vast knowledge of the Bible and make it a lot of fun, and do it in such a way that you weren't likely to forget it."

David had moved back to Fayetteville to be with his parents, who like so many others found out that their son was gay and that he was dying of AIDS at the same time. David's parents moved him into a mobile home on the back of their property, and his sister Pam moved in with him to become his caregiver. As with Allen, June came by once a week to give David communion and spend a few hours talking with him. On his thirtieth birthday, June brought him a ceramic bear to go with his collection of stuffed ones. "I look like I'm eighty," David complained to her. "Nonsense," June had responded. "Just because you're thin, that doesn't make you look old. You've still got that little kid's face."

Nancy Kepple was a member of the Community United Church of Christ. As we have seen, she was appointed to Raleigh's Commission on Human Resources and Human Relations in May of 1987 and subsequently persuaded it to tackle the thorny question of whether or not sexual orientation should be added to the city's nondiscrimination ordinance. When she found herself rounding up speakers for the upcoming hearing on the proposal, Reverend Norris was a natural person to invite. June told the commission about the threats and discrimination she had faced just for working with gays and lesbians. Afterward, she too became one of the founding members of the Raleigh Religious Network for Gay and Lesbian Equality.

The city council vote that followed the hearing was a major victory for gay men and lesbians in Raleigh. The formation of RRNGLE may have been an even more significant gain. But in the middle of 1987, it was hard to feel like celebrating. At the rate that people were dying, it sometimes seemed that there would be no one left to benefit from all of these advances.

When David Huggins died in July of 1987, the funeral arrangements were much the same as Allen's. Again no mention was made of the fact that David was gay or of what had killed him. Although all of David's close family knew that he had died of AIDS, they were afraid that their friends would shun them if the truth were more widely known. Once again there were two funerals: one for the man that his family thought David should have been, and one for the man that his friends knew he really was. June conducted the memorial service at St. John's on a Saturday. In the past six months, she had done twelve funerals. The next day she went down to Florida for MCC's General Conference.

"By that time, I had become numb. I got to the point where I felt like I couldn't cry, and I couldn't feel sorrow or happiness or anything. I was just so numb." When June arrived at the conference, she found out that two of her good friends and fellow clergy were close to death. Sometime at that conference, she began to cry.

June was still crying when she got back. A few days later, she was still crying. Those around her could see that she needed help, and her colleagues in the Cooperative Campus Ministry decided to step in. The campus ministers from several different denominations chipped in and sent June to a grief retreat at Kirkridge, Pennsylvania. As it happened, the retreat was run by Father John J. McNeill. He had been a Jesuit priest for forty years until his order expelled him for arguing against the Catholic church's condemnation of homosexuality.[5]

When June came back from Kirkridge, it became clear that she wasn't the only one who was upset. Attendance at St. John's Sunday worship services had dropped from a peak of about ninety down to sixty. The rumblings of dissatisfaction that had started in 1984 were by late 1987 becoming an open rift within the church. As is often the case, no one can now agree on exactly what the arguments were about. Although the church held a number of meetings and forums to try to discuss the problem, it seemed as if those who disagreed were talking past each other. Not only could they not agree with each other, they couldn't even agree on what they were disagreeing about in the first place.

June believes that there was no real disagreement, only a lot of unfocused rage over all the deaths in the congregation. She claims that the people who were the most angry with her were the very ones who had never volunteered any time to help out the AIDS patients that St. John's was caring for. She guesses that these were the people who were most afraid and upset, and that she became an outlet for their frustration.

Indeed, there were statements floating around St. John's such as, "If you want to get an appointment with June, you're going to have to develop AIDS first." It wasn't that anyone objected to helping people with AIDS. Rather, they felt that June wasn't managing her time very well, and was neglecting the day-to-day running of the church. Running off to hold someone's hand when he lives a hundred miles away might be compassionate, they argued, but it wasn't terribly efficient. Why not get a volunteer who actually lived in the area to care for the patient? Even June had to admit, "With all my AIDS ministry, I didn't have as much time to prepare services. I wasn't getting enough rest, and my preaching didn't have the same quality."

For many members of St. John's, though, the conflict had nothing to do with AIDS at all—it had to do with what the church was going to be. June's sermons were still focused generally on the theme of "It's OK to be gay, and God loves you just the way you are." And there had been a time when the members had needed to hear that message. But the gay community around St. John's had matured over the years. Having come to accept themselves, they were more interested in working for change in the world—and not necessarily just on gay issues. June's message was no longer enough for them. Wayne Lindsey explains, "There is more to being a church than that. If we are about being a church, then we need to be doing other things. . . . We need to be doing outreach to the gay and lesbian community, but also *beyond* the gay and lesbian community. We should do all the things a Christian church is called to do: feed the hungry, clothe the naked, heal the sick.

"But that's not what was heard. What was heard was, 'We don't need to be saying this anymore.' But what we were trying to say was, 'We need to be saying more. And this can be included in what we are saying, but it needs to be expanded.' "[6]

The more meetings and forums that St. John's held, the more polarized the two sides became, and the more they stopped trusting each other. The situation finally came to a head at the congregational meeting in

January of 1989. The members of the congregation present voted 21–20 not to renew June's contract as pastor of St. John's.

The result shocked everyone, including the members of the opposition who had voted it into effect. No one had thought that those opposed to June's pastorate would actually win. Under the church's by-laws, failure to renew a contract is not the same as dismissing a pastor—a new contract can be renegotiated. At the time, however, no one in the congregation was familiar with the finer points of the by-laws, and everyone assumed that June had been fired. The Board of Directors, which had strongly supported June, promptly resigned en masse and left the church.

Although June was without a job by the end of January, she decided to put off leaving until the end of May. "For some reason, I just knew that I wasn't to leave there. I didn't understand it myself, except that I wasn't quite ready to leave yet."

June's hairdresser, Russell Williams, had resigned his membership in St. John's the night that June's contract had been dropped. His brother, Michael, had been diagnosed with AIDS several months earlier, and June had been to visit him several times.

"Michael was admitted to the hospital early in May, and then I knew why I was supposed to be there. He had pneumocystis. And I knew that Michael didn't really need me. Michael was very self-assured. He knew where his spirit was. He was OK. But he wanted me to minister to his mother. So I sat with his mother in the waiting room of intensive care throughout most of May. And when Michael died, it was so hard. . . .

"And then Russell told me that he was also beginning with AIDS. And he was so mad at the church, because I wouldn't be able to be there for him, when he died."

A few days later, Dixie flew into Raleigh and rented a moving van. Fourteen people from St. John's turned out to help June pack all of her belongings into it. Russell came by and insisted on giving them both perms before they left. June waved good-bye, and then she and her daughter started driving west, back to California.

St. John's had its share of problems after June left. With the entire board gone, there was no continuity of leadership. No one knew how things were supposed to be run. By April, the new board had asked Wayne Lindsey if he would fill in as temporary pastor, but they couldn't even agree on what his title should be. Wayne told them, "If you can't figure what to call it, I'm not going to do it."

A month later, the board finally agreed on the title "Pastoral Leader," and Wayne accepted the new position. Because Wayne was just a temporary fill-in, he spent most of the first year lining up different speakers to preach each Sunday. Unfortunately, the new faces in the pulpit every week contributed to a general feeling of instability, and attendance continued plummeting throughout the year until it hit rock bottom at about twenty people a week.

By January of 1990, the board had still not found a new pastor, and it asked Wayne if he would provide a little continuity by keeping office hours and preaching every other Sunday. Wayne was absolutely terrified by the idea of delivering a sermon. He talked it over with Mahan Siler, the pastor of Pullen Baptist, whom he knew from RRNGLE meetings.

"What do I have to say that anyone would want to hear?" he asked.

"I think it would be a good idea if more preachers felt that way," responded Siler with a chuckle. "But I think you need to look at this, because your community sees something that you don't. They have said, 'We want to hear a word from you.' You have to look at that as a real call in the context of community."

Wayne did manage to struggle through his first few sermons, and St. John's slowly got back on its feet. Eventually, the board decided that what it was looking for was exactly what it already had, and Wayne became the full-time pastor. He still finds preaching to be the hardest part of his work.

"To every week get up in front of 120 people and try to say something that is in some way *relevant* to where they live, and not just some 'pie-in-the-sky, by and by, won't it be great when we all get to heaven, Rah! Rah!'—that remains the biggest challenge I have every week."

Wayne thinks that St. John's has learned a lot from the old conflict. He makes a point now of delegating as much work as possible, so that the church develops as a community that can handle its own affairs rather than having one person take on all the responsibilities. He's also trying to help the congregation learn how to handle its disagreements better.

"People come into church a lot of times and they get swept away and caught up in it. And it's a wonderful experience, it really is. But they think, 'Oh, well, I have just died and gone to heaven, and this is the perfect place, and nothing could ever go wrong here.' And I make sure that I tell them in membership class that this is a *human* organization, and people make mistakes, and we get upset and angry with each other.

"If you come here expecting that this is going to be a perfect place, then you're going to have that expectation shattered. So I try my best to shoot it down from the beginning and say, 'Don't expect this. Help us. Learn how to struggle together.'

"If we can teach people how to fight with one another as they go along, and be honest, so that they're struggling and working together, then you don't ever get to that boiling-over point. I've been there once, and I don't ever want to go back there again."

In 1993 St. John's made a down payment on a building of its own, and moved out of the Community United Church of Christ, its host for so long. That same year, the MCC denomination applied for membership in the North Carolina Council of Churches. The council is an ecumenical organization that pools the resources of many denominations to work for charitable and social justice causes.

The MCC application was extensively debated at the council's May meeting. Of approximately sixty-five delegates, only two openly argued that MCC should be excluded because homosexuality is sinful. A more politic motion was made to delay the vote on MCC's membership until a study could conclude whether sexuality is a "legitimate organizing principle" for a church. Many of the delegates interpreted this motion as a stalling tactic. "What is a legitimate organizing principle for a church, anyway?" they asked. The council contains denominations that were formed because people felt the need for a black church, denominations that were formed to provide a religious justification for slavery, and denominations that were formed over disagreements about how much water it takes to properly baptize someone.

The motion to admit MCC to membership in the council was passed by a three-to-one margin, with some vocal dissenters. Shortly thereafter, the North Carolina Methodist Conference sent a letter stating that it would withold all support from the council and would not return until the MCC was expelled.

The Reverend Jimmy Creech, by now a program associate with the council, wasn't surprised by the Methodists' action. He does, however, think that it may backfire. "This is a decision that will come back to haunt the Methodists. Over the next few years, as the council is working and struggling with important social issues, the Methodists will be conspicuously absent. And eventually they are going to have to deal with all this."

The Reverends Jimmy Creech, Mahan Siler, and Jim Lewis, marching in the 1988 NC Gay and Lesbian Pride Parade—the event that initially brought Reverend Creech into conflict with the older members of his church. (Photo: *The Front Page* [Raleigh], June 5–18, 1990, p. 1)

Kevin Turner and Steven Churchill at their wedding reception.

Mike and Catherine Watts.

John Blevins at Olin T. Binkley
Memorial Baptist Church.

Richard Bardusch outside Duke
Chapel.

The Reverend Jim Lewis

The Reverend June Norris of the Metropolitan Community Church.

Roxanne Seagraves (right) and Cris South, at their wedding reception outside Chapel Hill Friends Meeting House.

CHAPTER 7

The Quaker Process: Chapel Hill Friends Meeting

Charlotte, North Carolina. In 1969, Cris South graduated from high school and got married. She was nineteen at the time. "In that age, that's what girls did when they graduated from high school," she explains. It was even true for girls who knew that they would rather be with other women.

"Oh, I questioned it. But I really wanted to be acceptable. And I was really, truly running away from who I was and what I was. And so I did the best I could.

"I had known since I was a teenager. But it was not an acceptable way to be. There was no big gay rights movement. Stonewall happened in the sixties, but I was totally out of contact in the South. I didn't know any gay people—men or women. And everything that I had been raised to believe in said that it was perverted and very, very wrong. Of all the things in the world that you could be, that was the worst. My mother rated it below prostitution, which was pretty low.

"I came from a very working-class Southern family, and there were levels at which you could descend the ladder. Poor white trash was one, and dating blacks was another, so there were lots of taboos. And this one rated down at the bottom of the barrel.

"In fact, I wanted to go to college, and my folks couldn't afford to send me, and I was thinking seriously about joining the military in order to get into the college fund. And my parents absolutely forbade me to do it, because only lesbians and poor white trash women joined the military."

At the time of her marriage, Cris had never actually had sex with another woman. She only knew that she wanted to. Still, she thought it only fair to be honest with her future husband.

"He was very understanding. His thought was that it made me much more of a whole person. His feeling was that a lot of people had those feelings but were desperately afraid of them. Because I acknowledged mine in some ways, I was less afraid of who I was as a total person."

Two years into their marriage, their son, Spence, was born. Cris tried very hard to be a good wife. To cure her lesbianism, she turned to religion. "I figured if I just put my life on track, and got right with God, and got married, and had children, and did all the right things, it would go away. If I never acted on it, it wouldn't become real."

Cris's desire to "get right with God" grew more and more intense over the next few years. She decided that the Methodist church wasn't meeting her spiritual needs and left to become a Lutheran. The Lutheran church that she joined was a part of the charismatic movement—they believed in modern-day miracles, speaking in tongues, and faith healings. Cris joined the ranks of "born again" Christians, and even worked for the Billy Graham Crusade for a while. But the more intensely Cris became involved in organized religion, the more disillusioned she became with it.

"The thing that finally turned me off was that I was chastised by so many people for being outspoken. I really believed that I had a mission and a place. And I was constantly being *put* in my place by people quoting the Bible to me about how Paul said women shouldn't minister to men, and women should be meek, and women shouldn't speak in church—and I finally said, 'To hell with this! Whatever this is, I have no place in it.'

"And it was a very painful tearing away—realizing that what I had experienced in several different denominations of organized religion really had no place for who I truly was, even in my straight guise. Not to mention the fact that the lesbianism was becoming more and more a factor in my life. I was finding it harder to ignore that part of me, although I still hadn't acted on it at that point. I was very unhappy in my marriage, very unhappy in the church.

"I was practically suicidal at that point, because I felt like there was no place for me, there was no acceptable, OK place to be in the world."

In 1976, at the age of twenty-six, Cris walked away from organized religion altogether. Sinking into a deep depression, she didn't leave her house for several months.

By 1977 Cris was at least able to leave her own home, and one of her closest friends invited her to a party down in Columbia, South Carolina. Although she had known the woman for some time, Cris had only recently learned that she was a lesbian. Cris's husband warned her not to go, saying that he knew exactly what kind of party it was going to be. But Cris decided to go anyway.

It was at that party that Cris finally realized that she wasn't alone in the world, that there were lots of lesbians around, and that they came in every size and shape imaginable. There were butch trucker lesbians at the party, there were lesbians who could have walked off the pages of a fashion magazine, and there were even lesbians who looked like suburban house-wives. Cris and her husband separated a month later.

At the time, Spence was six years old. In those days, it was almost always the case that the mother got custody of the children—unless the mother was a lesbian. Cris's husband assured her that he would bring this fact up if they ended up in a court battle.

"He threatened me with taking away my son. And I finally had to reach the point where I wasn't going to let that be a factor that kept me in the marriage anymore. And he did eventually take my son away from me.

"About six months later he got custody, because I was not willing to make my son a pawn in a big custody battle in court. I just gave him custody because I couldn't put my six-year-old through that."

Initially, Cris was awarded "father's" visitation rights. After a few con-versations between their lawyers, however, her former husband agreed that Spence needed more contact with his mother, and he loosened up the visitation rights considerably.

After her separation, Cris began making friends in Charlotte's gay and lesbian community. A few of the people that she met had been reading about two new religious organizations: the Metropolitan Community Church, a new denomination for gay men and lesbians, and Dignity, an organiza-tion of gay Roman Catholics that was growing rapidly. Cris put in a lot of time and effort to help establish an MCC church in Charlotte, but it never quite got off the ground. The Dignity chapter was more successful, and

Cris started attending their masses. "But again," she says, "it didn't fit. Because it was Catholic, and I wasn't."

In 1978 she drove to Raleigh several times to attend St. John's MCC. Although she did eventually move to nearby Durham, she chose not become a member of St. John's. Again, it just didn't fit.

In the early 1980s, Cris met a group of women who practiced Goddess worship and Wicca, a pre-Christian matriarchal form of nature worship. "I tried it for a while, and it didn't fit. I wanted it to desperately, because I was a very strong feminist. But it didn't. Although I did a lot of rituals with women, and a few that had some men included, that were very powerful and very affirming, there was some kind of spiritual need in me that this didn't satisfy. There was like an empty hole. And I kept trying to find things to fill it up. And worshiping trees and doing dances around fires and all didn't do it. There needed to be something more there. And so I just kind of wrote it off, and just learned to live with that empty feeling for a number of years."

Greensboro, North Carolina. In 1984 Roxanne Seagraves was just out of school, just out of the closet, and right in the middle of a crisis of faith. Roxanne was a devout member of the Religious Society of the Friends of Truth, also known as Quakers. She was on the Coordinating Committee for the World Gathering of Young Friends, which was to take place at Guilford College in 1985. Roxanne had been working closely with the other committee members for months, and like most of her friends, they knew that she was a lesbian. Personally, they had no problem with that. They were worried that other Friends might, however.

"There was pressure from the rest of the Coordinating Committee for me to stand aside as a lesbian. I could stand with them as a Quaker, but I couldn't stand with them as a lesbian Quaker. Their concern was that having me as a lesbian coordinator of this group, even though I was a Friend, would alienate and create hostilities between Evangelical Friends, Friends from Kenya, Friends from Guatemala, Friends from Mexico, Friends from Madagascar. They thought that when all these Friends from around the world came together and they saw me, an openly gay person on the Coordinating Committee, that it would create immediate divisiveness among the Friends gathered. So they asked me to be silent on the issue of my sexuality." For Roxanne, who took the name of her religion seriously, this was a lot to ask.

"I had an enormous crisis of faith, because I felt like I was being asked to participate in a spiritual gathering as a liar. And I felt that one can't lie to God if one is to be truly a part of the spiritual community. One can't be in a relationship and be a liar."

Roxanne decided that truth was not a virtue she could afford to compromise. She did not attend the World Gathering that she herself had helped to plan. From that point on she decided that she was going to be absolutely open about her sexuality. She came out to everyone in her home congregation, Chapel Hill Friends Meeting, and they continued to welcome and support her.

A few years earlier, in 1981, two women who were members of University Friends Meeting in Seattle had asked to be married under the care of their meeting. Their marriage committee arrived at clearness on the wisdom of the union, and the meeting was preparing to move on and plan the wedding. One Friend stood up, however, and said that he couldn't accept the use of the word "marriage" for such a ceremony. "Marriage" had a special, sacred meaning to him, and he could not accept its being used for a lesbian relationship. Rather than deadlock over a single work, the meeting substituted the term "ceremony of commitment," and the union took place. It is the first known instance of a Quaker meeting celebrating a same-sex relationship.

The term "ceremony of commitment" was subsequently adopted by a number of other meetings that were also facing requests for same-sex unions. In 1982 one ceremony of commitment was performed under the care of another meeting in the United States, and in 1983 one was performed by Transvaal Friends Meeting in South Africa. In 1985 three other meetings performed ceremonies of commitment. In 1986, an additional three meetings passed minutes stating their willingness to perform such ceremonies.

Nineteen eighty-seven was a busy year. Three meetings celebrated ceremonies of commitment. In addition, Morningside Friends Meeting held the first *marriage* for two gay men ever performed at a Quaker meeting. By the end of the year, four other meetings had followed suit, *marrying* three lesbian couples and one gay male couple. One of these meetings, North Meadow Circle of Friends, explained why it thought the use of the word "marriage," with all its sacred implications, was so important. "We learned that terminology is more than just words; it can evoke pain and prolong oppression."

In 1988, in an extremely unusual move for Quakers, the Western Yearly Meeting expelled North Meadow Circle of Friends until such time as they reversed their decision on allowing gay and lesbian couples to use the word "marriage."[1]

Cris and Roxanne met for the first time in 1987. It wasn't until 1989, though, that they began to spend much time together. They were both hanging out at a bookstore called Southern Sisters, and fell into talking. They discovered that they had a lot to talk about. They were both interested in spirituality, about how people relate to God and how they use their religion in their daily lives. They were also both artists: Cris had become a painter and Roxanne was a sculptor, as well as a professional storyteller. The two of them began spending a great deal of time with each another— praying together, shooting pool, camping. And talking. Just a lot of wonderful conversations.

This is what Roxanne brings up most often when she tries to explain their relationship. "We love to talk. Cris and I have wonderful conversations about any variety of subjects. We're both people who enjoy exploring the world, and looking at it.

"Cris and I are very different in our approaches to that exploration. Cris loves to say, 'OK, this is my ten acres, let me see what's in it.' I love to say, 'Look, this is my ten acres, let me see what's outside it.' Run run run, jump the fence is my first move. And then I'll come back to Cris and she'll say, 'Look at all the stuff that was here!' And I'll say 'Look at all the stuff that was out there!' We have a wonderful relationship because we both get pictures of the whole through each other."

At the time that Cris and Roxanne met, neither of them was looking for a lover. It wasn't until they'd already been friends for about six months that they realized what they had they found in each other. They made love for the first time on Christmas Day, 1989.

Cris knew a little bit about the Society of Friends, and had liked what she'd heard. "The fact that they did not separate working for the good of society, working for the good of humankind, working for civil rights, from the way they worshiped was very appealing to me."

Still, Cris had had quite enough of organized religion by that point. Roxanne kept asking her to come to meeting each Sunday, and each Sunday, Cris would find an excuse not to go. But, Cris ran out of excuses before Roxanne ran out of persistence, and she agreed to go one Sunday. Cris was in for a surprise. Roxanne belongs to the traditional, nonprogrammed branch of Friends, and their services are unlike anything in mainstream Protestantism.

The basic belief of the Society of Friends is that there is that of God within every person. Thus Friends don't believe that they need a minister or a ritual through which to hear the word of God. They need only sit in silence, listening for the voice of God within themselves, and really listening when that voice moves another member to break the silence and speak. At a Friends meeting, the pews don't face an altar, they face each other.

Her first meeting for worship made a big impression on Cris. "Quakerism is a very inclusive way of having a religion. Finally I went to a meeting with Roxanne, and was stunned at the differences in the people there. Now there were people who did read and believe the Bible, literally, and took great comfort in the Bible. We would have people get up and give a message about Paul, and then another person would get up and give some thoughts about having just read something by Mao Tse-tung. It was very eclectic. And there was this firm belief that the Spirit was as individualized as the individual. So there was this huge amount of acceptance of differences in where people came from and how each one believed.

"I think that's one of the reasons I love Quakerism: it's anarchy in action. It's the one place in the world that I've found where people honestly believe that our differences are our strengths."

Cris began attending meeting with Roxanne on a regular basis. She did not go in the "every Sunday, rain or shine" way that Roxanne went, but a good two or three times a month. After all, meeting isn't something you do because you're supposed to. It is something you do because you want to, when you feel the need for it.

In the early summer of 1990, Cris popped the question to Roxanne. She knew, of course, that the state of North Carolina wouldn't grant them a marriage license, but Cris wanted some sort of celebration of their love, a statement of their commitment to help each other through the rough times. Cris had known many lesbian couples who had gone off in the woods together and conducted a New Age–style ceremony. At first, that's all that she envisioned for Roxanne and herself.

Roxanne, however, felt that a wedding is as much about community as it is about the couple. It's about speaking your love in front of your friends and family, your community of faith, and having them witness it. For Roxanne, her community of faith was her meeting. As she remembers it, "I stalled. I wasn't direct about it, I just stalled. And finally, after three months of my stalling every time Cris brought it up, she said, 'Do you want to do this in the meeting house?'

"And I said, 'Yes, that's the only place I want to do it.' "

Cris and Roxanne had assumed that Chapel Hill Friends Meeting would handle their request for marriage in exactly the same way that it would handle any heterosexual couple's. After all, Chapel Hill Meeting had been supportive and gay-friendly for a number of years. The meeting had held discussion groups on gay and lesbian issues as early as 1978, and in the mid-1980s had passed a minute, a sort of resolution, formally supporting basic civil rights for gay men and lesbians. There were several members of the meeting who were openly gay. When the meeting had rewritten its marriage document in 1988, it had carefully left the wording gender neutral, in case the meeting should one day decide to marry a same-sex couple.

Cris and Roxanne composed a letter explaining the love they had for each other and asking to be married under the care of the meeting.

As is often the case, what happened next depends on whom you talk to. As Ann Riggs, the clerk of the Overseers Committee, remembers it, she was coming into meeting one Sunday when Martha Gwyn, the clerk of meeting, came rushing up to her.

"There's a letter in your mailbox," Martha told Ann. "We knew it was coming sometime, and now it's here."

At the time, Riggs had a disturbing problem on her mind. A homeless person with severe emotional problems had been hanging around the meeting house, and the Overseers Committee had been trying to come up with a compassionate solution to the problem before someone got hurt. When she heard about the letter, Riggs was terrified that it was going to report a death, an attack, or at least some horrible misunderstanding.

Thus Ann remembers being relieved when she opened the letter and discovered that it was only a request by two women for marriage under the care of the meeting. She recalls calmly phoning them to discuss the ramifications of their request.

Roxanne remembers things a bit differently. "We got a panicked phone call from Ann Riggs, saying, 'You know you can't just do this! There's no precedent for this. You know that we're going to have to change the marriage document. You know there could be a lot of problems with this.'

"And Cris and I sort of looked at each other and said, 'Yeah, we do know this.' "

Quaker organization follows naturally from their belief that there is that of God within each person. Just as they see no need for a minister to tell them the word of God, they also see no need for bishops, district coordinators, or General Conventions. Each Quaker meeting functions as an independent entity, responsible only to the conscience of its members for the decisions that it makes.

Furthermore, there is no hierarchy within the meeting. Rather than having leaders, Quaker meetings have clerks. The clerks serve not to make decisions but to facilitate discussion among the members. They call meetings to order, dismiss them, and attempt to put words to the "sense of the meeting" that emerges from discussion. Judy Purvis, the clerk of the Ministry and Worship Committee, explains, "Among nonprogrammed Friends, the need to have power in a meeting is looked upon as mildly weird. Playing politics has nothing to do with quietly sitting down and trying to discern the will of God."

The method by which a Quaker meeting arrives at "clearness" on a decision is quite different from the decision-making processes in other churches. When you believe that there is that of God within everyone, you must carefully listen to every person. Not just to what the majority thinks, but to every single person. As Friends see it, no one sees the whole truth, but each of us can see a part of it. So by coming together, we can see it more clearly. The lone holdout who doesn't agree with the rest of the meeting on an issue may simply see a part of the truth that no one else has grasped yet. It is as important for the meeting to listen carefully to him as it is for him to listen carefully to the rest of meeting.

Thus Quaker arguments tend to look a lot like their meetings for worship. Friends sit in silence, periodically broken by one of them who feels moved to speak on the issue. Then they return to silence, to think about what has been said, to see if it expands their understanding of the truth, and to try to discern the will of God. This continues until everyone agrees on the matter or until the remaining dissenters "stand aside"— essentially saying that although they don't agree with the decision, they do not feel spiritually led to prevent the meeting from moving forward with it.

The clearness process means that when a decision is finally reached, it enjoys a remarkable amount of support from the members. The problem is that Quaker meetings can sometimes take years to arrive at clearness on a controversial issue. When there are strong feelings on both sides of the issue, the process can be indefinitely deadlocked. Sometimes, when the holdouts are older members, meetings have been known to resolve a problem by simply waiting for the dissenters to die of old age.

When Ann Riggs presented the letter to the Overseers Committee, she quickly discovered that there was not yet clearness on the issue of marrying two women. In fact, the overseers were worried that this sort of issue could cause a rift in the meeting. They asked if this was a serious request, or just some sort of gay publicity stunt. They asked if Cris and Roxanne were really talking about the same kind of lifetime commitment that heterosexual marriage entailed. And they asked why it had to be called a marriage. For many of them, the word had a strong meaning, and a part of that meaning was that it took place between a man and a woman.

The Overseers Committee eventually decided that there were three things that needed to happen before a wedding could take place. First, the meeting as a whole would have to come to clearness on being willing to perform a same-sex marriage. Second, Roxanne and Cris would go through a clearness process led by a marriage committee, just as any straight couple would. Last, someone would have to figure out the legal ramifications of marrying two women in the state of North Carolina.

The process of clearness for marriage is unique to the Society of Friends. In some ways it resembles the premarital counseling performed by ministers in other denominations, although it is a great deal more thorough and in-depth. In Quaker parlance, couples are not married *by* a meeting. They are married *under the care of* the meeting. This means that the community takes an active role in supporting the marriage and has a responsibility to see that it is well advised in the first place. The Clearness Committee meets with the couple and asks them a number of detailed queries: What do they expect from the relationship? What do they expect from a spouse? How do they plan to handle issues of money, power, sexuality, control, children? The process can go on for months, until both the committee and the couple are satisfied that they are ready to take this step in their relationship. In one case at Chapel Hill Friends, the couple and the committee met every month for a full two years before all the issues had been resolved.

The committee for Roxanne and Cris's marriage wound up being a bit larger than usual, with seven members. The Overseers Committee was being especially careful, making sure that there were members on board to handle any possible problems. Bill Flash, for example, was selected because of personal experiences with clearness committees for his own marriages.

"The first one was just perfunctory," he says, "and should never have happened. It was laden with the expectations of the parents, and no attention was paid to us as prospective married people. We were married in an old meeting in which our parents were quite active, so the Clearness Committee said, 'Of course!' and no questions were asked."

The Clearness Committee for Bill's second marriage had been a much longer and, he feels, more useful affair. The committee asked about everything, including how his prospective wife would relate to his ex-wife and his children. It took a great deal of time and effort, but Bill feels that the process did a lot to lay a good foundation for his new marriage. "It helps a lot to have someone outside yourselves asking the embarrassing, difficult questions."

Elisa Jones was selected for Cris and Roxanne's Clearness Committee because she is a lesbian. She had come out to the meeting back in 1978, and the Overseers believed that she would be able to look at this relationship more critically than anyone else. While everyone was concentrating on the fact that this was a relationship between two women, Elisa would be looking at whether or not it was a *good* relationship. As Ann Riggs put it, "I didn't know Cris that well. And I had some rather protective feelings about Roxanne. Who is she marrying? Who is this person she just dragged in out of nowhere? We put Cris through hell, to find out if she was up to snuff."

Then there was Henry Cobb, who joined the Clearness Committee for his own reasons. Henry had some real discomfort with the idea of two women getting married, and he wanted to work through it. Cris explains, "He had known Roxanne through the meeting for some time. But he was eighty-two years old, and had not had that much contact with gay people, and had just been raised to believe that this was not a normal, healthy way of life. He had rejected a lot of that intellectually. But getting your heart and your head to agree on something—that's difficult.

"Henry loved Roxanne, he thought that she was a wonderful human being. As he told us, 'There was something that I needed to learn, and something that I needed to unlearn.' "

Roxanne comments, "He did it without making Cris and me feel that we were responsible for his feelings, or that his feelings bore more weight than his concern for our marriage."

The Clearness Committee began meeting with Cris and Roxanne on October 1, 1990.

Shortly after the Clearness Committee was chosen, a group of people got together to decide how the matter should be presented to the meeting as a whole. Judy Purvis was one of them.

"That small committee asked the question, 'How do we introduce this topic to the community in a way that gives people a chance to think about it without having to get rushed into a decision? Because when you rush people into a decision, if they're uncomfortable about it, it tends to harden their position. You need to give them time, you need to give people space to explore how they feel, and how other people feel."

Judy had come from a meeting in Cleveland that had become deadlocked over exactly this issue. Two women who had been members of the meeting for years asked to be married. Eight years later, that meeting was still struggling with the request. All but two members were in agreement that the marriage process should proceed, but those remaining two members were adamant in their position and did not feel that they could stand aside in good conscience. The two women's request had thus never been answered.

The committee at Chapel Hill Friends decided that the issue should be discussed in every small group within the meeting: the Wednesday morning women's group, the young Friends' group, the Finance Committee, the men's group, the Religious Education Committee, the Public Issues Committee, and so on.

"Any kind of gathering of Friends," said Judy, "we asked that they explore the issue. And we asked that they do it not from [a] 'What should we do?' [perspective] but just let people sort of ventilate about how they felt about the issue. We figured that would provide a forum for people to check out where they were in relation to other people in an informal context and allow people to share information, allow them to ask questions of each other, and that would keep people from feeling threatened. If we raised the issue for the first time in a business meeting, people might feel a lot shyer about expressing concerns or difficulties.

"And we were concerned. Because we are a fairly liberal community, we knew that most people would be fairly comfortable with the idea. We were afraid that the people who weren't comfortable would not feel OK about expressing their concerns, or, because of the pressure, would express them in harder terms than they felt."

The small groups were asked to consider the issue of same-sex marriage in the light of bigger questions: Why do we celebrate marriage in the first place? How do we judge whether a relationship is good or bad? What does it really mean for two people to married?

The people in the small groups expressed many of the same concerns that had been expressed in the Overseers Committee. Because Roxanne belonged to some of the small groups, she took part in several of the discussions. During one meeting, a woman asked Roxanne if she was just doing this to promote the gay rights agenda. "After all," she said, "it's not like you're going to have children."

Roxanne looked at the woman in disbelief and pointed to two members of the meeting who had been married in their late fifties, well past child-bearing age. "Well, why did they get married if they weren't going to have children?" As Roxanne saw it, marriage wasn't about securing property rights to children anymore. It was about love and commitment and wanting to spend the rest of your life with a person.

Other people worried that if they approved this gay marriage, then the meeting would be swamped with homosexuals wanting to get married. Roxanne laughed at that suggestion.

"If you've ever been through the process of clearness for membership and then clearness for marriage," she says, "you know that it's a major chore. Few people would go through with it when you could just go out and spit over your shoulder and get as much legal support."

There were also a few people who objected specifically to the use of the word "marriage." They didn't have any problem with two women celebrating their love, but to them marriage was a sacred institution that could only exist between a man and a woman.

For their part, the Overseers were also worried about what the state of North Carolina might have to say about the use of the word "marriage." First off, it was highly unlikely that the state would issue Cris and Roxanne a marriage license. And under the general statutes of North Carolina, it is a misdemeanor offense, punishable by up to two years in prison, for anyone to marry a couple without first obtaining a marriage license.

There was also the problem of North Carolina General Statute 14-177, the so called "Crimes against Nature" law. The statute uses vague language dervied from a law first drafted by Henry VIII. In its current form, it reads, "If any person shall commit the crime against nature, with mankind or beast, he shall be punishable as a class H felon." The state had never defined what the "crime against nature" is, so it was impossible to tell if Chapel Hill Friends would be violating the statute by marrying two women. In practice, the law means whatever the prosecuting attorney wants it to. The "crime against nature" has at various times been held to mean sex between people of the same sex, sex in a public place, or prostitution.

After consulting a couple of legal experts in the meeting, the Overseers Committee concluded that the probability that anyone at Chapel Hill Friends would be prosecuted for the marriage was exceedingly slim. The simple problem of figuring out whom to prosecute would be enough to drive any district attorney to distraction. As with all Friends services, the marriage ceremony is conducted by the entire meeting, without the need for a minister. It was difficult to imagine the state trying to prosecute all of the fifty or so members who would attend the wedding and sign the marriage document. Joe Dipierro summed it up in his memo to the committee, "It would be a difficult case and not worth a prosecutor's time."

The political ramifications of conducting the wedding were a quite different matter, however. In North Carolina, the right of Quaker meetings to marry couples without a minister is legislated in one particular clause of the general statutes. It was all too easy to imagine an angry state legislature revoking that clause. Such an action would affect every Friends meeting in the state.

As far as Ann Riggs was concerned, that was just fine. Quaker marriages had started off as purely spiritual affairs anyway, with no legal implications. Why should the state be involved in telling churches whom they can and can't marry? Quakers have a long tradition of standing up to governments on matters of moral principle. Quakers had helped slaves escape north on the underground railroad in the 1800s. Quakers had refused to be drafted because of their belief in peace. When it came down to a decision between what was legal and what they believed to be right, Quakers had traditionally chosen to violate the law rather than their own principles.

Others on the Overseers Committee were less sanguine about this course of action. They were willing to rock the boat for a good cause, but as Ann says, "Nobody wanted to rock the boat for every other meeting in the state without even trying to contact them."

In the Society of Friends, everything is done according to the same process by which they hope to find the truth. Thus they do not have separate meetings for worship and for business. Instead they have a monthly meeting for worship with attention to business.

It was at such a meeting in January of 1991 that Cris and Roxanne's marriage committee reported that they had reached clearness on the wisdom of this marriage. That statement said a great deal to the other members of the meeting.

"The people who were chosen to be on it were very weighty people in the meeting," explained Ann Riggs, "people who could be expected to not just go, 'Oh yes, this is wonderful,' but to really think the whole thing through, to ask hard questions, and to have good reasons for making the decision they did."

It also mattered that Cris and Roxanne were not, in Judy Purvis's words, "dismissible people." Roxanne had been a member of the meeting for years, and people knew her well. She had contributed a great deal of time to the meeting—serving on committees for other people's memberships and marriages and visiting older or sick members who couldn't get out. Roxanne wasn't likely to do something like this for frivolous reasons, and it was hard for anyone to believe that she had been a good Quaker all these years just to stage some sort of protest marriage now. In the end, they all believed that she and Cris were simply looking for an honest celebration of their love.

That still left the divisive issue of what to call this celebration. Although there were several people who were ready to take on the state legislature for the right of same-sex couples to use the word "marriage," there were also many who didn't want to upset the other Quakers in the state by risking their right to perform legal marriages. And there were still some people who had a gut-level discomfort with using the word "marriage" to describe a lesbian relationship.

In the end, it was Cris who resolved the matter. She stood up and said, "Look, you don't fight every battle." The issue of same-sex marriages was likely to come before the state legislature within the next five years, but it wasn't likely to be resolved for another twenty. For now, it was enough to have the ceremony, and not fight a political battle for the use of a word. "We can live with the term 'holy union.' "

With that, the meeting quickly came to clearness on the issue of performing same-sex unions. Although it is rarely the case with controversial subjects, the resolution was absolutely unanimous—not one person stood aside.

A few weeks after that decision, Judy Purvis found herself being chewed out by a woman in the supermarket who believed the word "marriage" should have been used and who accused her of being "unwilling to speak truth to power." Judy still feels that the meeting made the right choice, however. "If we had been the only ones affected, we might have been willing to speak truth to power. But did we have the right to speak for all the other meetings in the state?"

Shortly after the decision, Cris became ill, and the ceremony had to be delayed for more than a year. It finally took place on a beautiful Sunday in July of 1992.

"We may have called it a 'holy union' because of legalities in the state of North Carolina," says Cris, "but Roxanne and I got married, and everyone in the meeting called it a wedding, and called it a marriage, and we wear rings, and I don't consider myself any less married to her than when I was married to Jim."

The ceremony was simple, like most Quaker weddings. No elaborate gowns, no tuxedos, no frills. Cris and Roxanne's friends gathered in the meeting house to sit in silence with them, periodically speaking out to wish them well, to say how much they loved them, or to say how happy they were that the two of them had found each other. One couple sang. Someone read from the Book of Ruth. One person tried to explain how wonderful it was that Cris and Roxanne had come together.

"You, Roxanne, are like water, that bubbles and ripples. And you, Cris, are like a forest—still and deep, with sunlight pouring down. I love you both, and I am so happy for you."

After an hour, Cris and Roxanne stood up and recited their vows to each other. They'd written them out ahead of time, but when the moment came, they both felt the need to improvise. I still remember a part of Roxanne's vow.

"Accept me. Accept that I need to laugh sometimes just to keep myself from crying. And accept that I need to cry sometimes, just to keep myself from laughing."

After the wedding, everyone gathered outside for the reception. Someone asked Roxanne if her family was there. At that moment her father, Jim Seagraves, was in Oregon campaigning for a congressional seat on a staunchly antigay "family values" platform. He often bragged to voters about his successful marriage of twenty-five years. As Roxanne's mother would point out, however, it was only successful because they had been divorced for the last fifteen of them. On the day of the wedding, Helen Seagraves was also in Oregon, campaigning for gay rights and against her former husband.

Looking around at the reception, at her friends and her meeting, Roxanne answered, "Well, no. Not from my biological family. But my family is *all here*."

Looking back, Judy Purvis wonders whether this was an issue that Chapel Hill Friends should have grappled with in advance, or whether they were right to wait for "that letter that we always knew was coming."

"There's always a problem when the subject comes up this way. It's helpful in some ways when a meeting can consider the issue of same-sex marriage separate from a particular petition, because then you don't get into personalities. The disadvantage, at least as I've seen it in other meetings, is that there is no particular impetus to get the thing resolved, because there isn't anybody waiting around for you to have a decision. Meetings usually don't grapple very successfully with the issue until somebody pushes them a little bit, until there is some reason why they actually have to come to clearness on it."

CHAPTER 8

A Challenge for the Process: Durham Friends Meeting

Bucks County, Pennsylvania, 1977. Like most Presbyterian boys, Jim Gilkeson began confirmation classes when he was thirteen. He received instruction in the set of beliefs that Presbyterians are expected to adhere to if they want to become full members of the church. Jim, however, came home after the second class and told his parents that he would not be continuing with it. Having learned what it meant to be a Presbyterian, he had decided that he was not one—he simply didn't believe in the doctrines they were teaching him. Jim's father was a bit concerned, but his mother realized that you can't force true faith, and so accepted his decision.

Jim's father was a firm believer in the value of a good education, and he was growing increasingly unhappy with the public school system in Bucks County. A third of the way through the school year, he pulled Jim out of the eighth grade and enrolled him in Lower Bucks Christian Academy, a private school run by Southern Baptists. It was an interesting, though not particularly agreeable, experience for Jim. His new science teacher talked about the dangers of believing in "Evil-lution," which he assured his students was a secular-humanist plot to lead them away from God's truth. In history, Jim was taught that the Indians had burned down whole forests to chase out the game, so that by driving the Indians off the white man had done a great service for the environment. And then there was the dress code, which was a particular puzzle for Jim. For some reason, the academy forbade anyone to wear a peace symbol. The teachers explained that the peace symbol represented a broken cross—surely a sign of great evil. Jim questioned them about this explanation several times. He knew from other sources that the peace sign was supposed to represent a dove's foot. He quickly found out, however, that the instructors at Lower Bucks Christian Academy did not enjoy being questioned: "It was all learning by rote. Education in their minds meant repeating back what was told to you. There was no tradition of questioning or figuring things out for yourself. Anything that questioned their truths was considered in some way evil."

At the end of the eighth grade, Jim left the academy. He had been accepted into George School, a Quaker high school five miles from his home. George School provided a very different educational experience. To begin with, Jim was encouraged to question everything. Nonprogrammed Friends have always been strong believers in intellectual freedom. Rather than telling their children what to believe, they ask them a series of questions designed to help them figure out the answers for themselves. They carry this attitude over into their schools. Jim was also surprised to find that no one tried to convert him. Nonprogrammed Friends don't proselytize—that is, they don't deliberately try to convince other people of their beliefs. Instead, they believe in "letting one's life speak." If what they are doing is good, then they figure that other people will eventually come to realize it. In Jim's case, this was true.

At first it was just that Jim liked the people. Although quite a few non-Friends attended George School, Jim found himself drawn to the students who had been raised in Quaker households. They were good people— they were friendly, they were interesting, and they truly seemed to care about what was going on in the world. Even when they argued they really listened to each other, and somehow the situation always got diffused short of violence. People simply didn't get into fights at George School. Jim came to respect the way that his friends carried their faith into their lives. These were people out searching for the truth, rather than waiting for someone else to hand it to them.

"That's what really attracted me to Quakerism in the first place: the notion that religion is not about finding this fixed set of prescriptions that someone sets down in front of you and then blanketly saying, 'I believe in all these things, and I will follow them.'—Well, the theory is that I will follow all these things. Or at least if I don't follow them I will feel very guilty and confess them to someone. And maybe even go through a regular cycle of sinning and confessing. It's not just in Catholicism that you get confession. We have Jimmy Swaggarts and Jim Bakkers who go through these cycles again and again, doing things that they preach against on Sunday, and getting caught, and then coming up with a great public confession.

"I came to have a strong aversion to the whole notion of Protestant churches, with the minister and programs each Sunday morning saying, 'Stand up now. Sit down now. Now hear this prayer. Now listen to this person tell you how to live. And then go home and do whatever you want because you're a good church member and you put something in the collection plate.' I just felt like most people in the church I grew up in only thought about religion to remember that it was time to go to church on Sunday."

By his senior year, Jim had become what is called a "convinced Friend," although he still did not consider himself to be a Christian. He had too many disagreements with the Christian church's teaching—a great deal of it seemed bigoted, or short-sighted, or simply based on cultural conditions that hadn't existed for two thousand years. Although Jim finds wisdom in the Bible, he also finds it in many other places. "My spiritual beliefs have nothing to do with Christianity," he says. "They would be just as appropriate for someone coming out of an Islamic, or Taoist, or Buddhist background. I am what is often termed a 'Universalist Friend'—one who believes that Quakerism is a universally acceptable road to the truth and that it shouldn't be based on a particular ethnic or social background."

In 1981 Jim graduated from George School and entered Duke University. Like many freshmen, he let his spiritual life take a backseat to the more immediate concerns of classes and a social life. A few weeks into the semester, though, he realized how much he missed meeting for worship at George School. He tracked down a local group of Quakers, Durham Friends Meeting, and began attending regularly. He quickly grew to love the meeting; much of what had drawn him to the Quakers at George

School now drew him to these people. Several months later Jim began the process of clearness for membership, whereby a committee of members meets with the candidate to discuss his or her faith and make sure that he or she understands Quaker philosophy and Quaker process. Jim became a member of Durham Friends Meeting in 1983 at the age of nineteen. It was the same year that he began coming to grips with the fact that he was gay.

During the 1980s, Durham Friends Meeting experienced a surge in membership as a number of young couples with children joined. One such couple was Don and Suzanne Markle.

Don had been raised in the Conservative Baptist denomination in eastern Oregon. When he moved to Alaska he joined a Congregational church, and it was in that church that he and Suzanne were married. Suzanne had been reading about the Society of Friends for several years, and was intrigued by their philosophy. When the couple moved to Durham in 1987, she decided that they should try several Quaker meetings, just to see what they were like. They went to Chapel Hill Friends Meeting several times, but eventually settled on Durham Friends, where they applied for membership.

Don had trouble with certain elements of the Quaker philosophy— they didn't seem to have any common creed, any rigid moral code, so it was hard to know if there was anything that they all agreed on. To Don, who was a strict believer in an inerrant Bible, some of the meeting's members seemed a bit far out. Don did enjoy the quiet contemplation of meeting for worship, however, and he liked the fact that anyone could help shape the course of the meeting. If you didn't like where the meeting was going, then you could always help turn it in a new direction.

Nineteen eighty-seven was also the year that Jim Gilkeson left Durham to pursue a master's degree at Georgia Tech. Atlanta had a strong and organized gay community, and during his time there Jim became involved in gay politics and the fight for basic civil rights.

By the time that Jim returned to Durham in 1989, he was thoroughly out of the closet. And although he was eager to begin attending Durham Meeting again, he didn't know how the other members would react to his sexuality. Jim spoke with several old friends, and they assured him that meeting would still be a welcoming place for him. In fact, they told him that there were now several other members who were out of the closet. Relieved, Jim came back to meeting. He also began teaching First Day school (Sunday school) for the high school students, as he had in the years before he left.

In the spring of 1990, Durham Friends Meeting set about rewriting its "Faith and Practice Document." The document lays out the traditions of the meeting: the procedure for being married under the care of the meeting, the procedure for becoming a member, and the procedure for celebrating a life (funerals). The document hadn't been updated since the 1950s, and there were a number of elements that needed to be revised to take account of changing times.

The minutes of Quaker "meetings for worship with attention to business" are kept anonymously, without reference to who made particular motions. What is considered important is the "sense of the meeting" on a subject, not keeping track of who said what to whom. As Friends like to explain it, they aspire to a process that is "truth driven" rather than "personality driven." John Hunter, who was participating in the discussions on revising the Faith and Practice Document, does recall, however, that it was a group of straight Friends who first brought up the subject of same-sex marriages.

At the time, Durham Friends Meeting had never been approached with a request for a gay or lesbian wedding. However, several people felt that it was only a matter of time before they were approached and that they needed to think about the issue before it happened.

As John Hunter remembers it, they figured, "We'd better be moving on this formally. Because although we have not been directly challenged, that time will come. And we would prefer to be ahead of it, rather than scrambling and having the first gay or lesbian couple asking for marriage be the guinea pigs, and make them feel horrible that they are the focus of this potentially rancorous process. It's better to deal with it ahead of time."

In the fall of 1990, Durham Friends Meeting held a series of forums to discuss the issue of same-sex marriage. Gilkeson and several other gay and lesbian members of the meeting devised a set of queries to guide the discussion. Jim explains, "We asked a set of five questions, which is how Quakers tend to give advice. You don't tell people what to think, you ask them questions that you hope will open them to think for themselves about something." The five questions were designed to draw out any fears and concerns that people might have about the meeting performing same-sex marriages.

1. Do we welcome couples of the same gender to apply for marriage under the care of the meeting?
2. Do we support gay and lesbian members/attenders and their families in the added struggles which they may face due to others' reactions to their sexual preference/orientation?
3. Do we appreciate the openness of lesbians & gay men who share their identities with us?
4. Do we provide gay and lesbian role models for the children in our meeting?
5. Do we welcome the notion that some of the children in our meeting will discover that they are lesbian or gay at some point in their lives?[1]

The issue of children was deliberately mentioned several times to make sure that anyone with concerns about this subject spoke up. Fundamentalists have often argued against gay rights by claiming that gay men are child molesters. In truth, the vast majority of child molesters are straight males, and usually the victim's relative or stepfather. Yet old stereotypes die hard.

The language of the queries was also carefully chosen. " 'Do we *welcome* something?' " explains Gilkeson. "Not, 'Do we tolerate it, do we put up with it and grit our teeth?' But do we actually welcome this and appreciate it?"

The goal of the forums was to get people to open up, to talk about their fears and discomforts. To a large extent they succeeded. The discussions on homosexuality were the best-attended forums that the meeting had ever held. Forums on most topics drew twelve to fifteen people. These had forty or fifty at each session.

After the forums, nothing was done on the subject for several months, and the issue of same-sex marriage was basically dropped. The subject was a controversial one about which many members had strong feelings, and it would be a difficult one for the meeting to work through. As a result, it appeared that Durham Friends Meeting was not going to grapple with the issue until it was absolutely forced to.

Jim Gilkeson, in particular, was upset by this lack of action. As he saw it, the meeting was "sitting around waiting until some gay or lesbian couple is brave enough to come forward and request marriage. And then they're going to be the test case. They're going to have to sit and hear their relationship talked about in ways that no one should have their relationship talked about when they've decided to be married, and they've asked to be married under the care of the meeting.

"This is something we should be able to talk about in the abstract and come to a decision on. So that the issue when a gay or lesbian couple asks to be married is not the fact that they are gay or lesbian, but the fact that they are a couple. And [as with] every other couple, the meeting wishes to assure itself that this marriage is well advised, before it takes it under its care."

As a member of Durham Friends Meeting, Jim hoped to one day be married under its care. "So I don't see this as just a theoretical point or a gay rights issue. I see this very personally. What are you saying to me about the status of my membership?" If members of the meeting saw his love, his relationship as somehow inferior to theirs, then was he really a member of this community?

Durham Friends Meeting meant a lot to Jim. He'd been an active member, serving on several committees in addition to teaching First Day school. After the meeting dropped the issue of same-sex marriage, however, Jim dropped the meeting. For eight months he avoided Durham Friends Meeting and the Sunday morning worship that had once meant so much to him.

Being away from meeting, though, only made Jim realize what an important part of his life it was. In the end, being a Quaker was too much a part of his identity for him to give it up. At the end of eight months he began attending meeting again, just going for Sunday morning worship and then leaving. Whereas before he would have stayed after worship to discuss meeting business or ask about people's families, now he left quietly without talking to anyone.

In April of 1992, Kathleen March, the clerk of the Ministry and Counsel Committee, drafted a new version of the marriage document and began circulating it to members of the meeting for comments. Like the revised marriage document that Chapel Hill Friends had put together a few years before, this one was carefully gender neutral, leaving the door open for the possibility of same-sex marriages without actually saying whether or not the meeting would be willing to perform them.

When Jim received his copy of the draft, he was offended by its ambiguous wording. He drafted a letter to Kathleen and the rest of the Ministry and Counsel Committee, explaining why he thought the meeting needed to settle this issue one way or the other. He wrote:

> As this issue is of personal concern to me, I am worried that my thoughts may be clouded by that closeness. I was only dimly becoming aware of my sexuality when I joined Durham Meeting in 1983. I was young, nineteen years old, at the time. "Coming out" and joining the Society of Friends were related events. Both were my expressions of figuring out who I was, one from a spiritual perspective and the other from a sexual one. However, my spiritual and sexual growth had yet to "meet" one another.
>
> I left Durham in 1987 to pursue a Master's degree in Atlanta. At that time, meeting was a very important part of my life. When I returned to Durham in 1989 to enter a graduate program in Finance, I found it hard to get back into the life of the meeting. Many of the new members were young, heterosexual, married couples; many had young children. "Family" seemed the emphasis, but with a traditionally narrow bent. Yet I returned with a greatly enhanced sense of wholeness. My sexuality had joined my faith as an outwardly expressed part of my identity.
>
> I have come to see in meeting in general, though a few people are exceptions, a marked discomfort with my sexuality. As was expressed at the 4/20/92 panel discussion on religion and homosexuality that we both attended, this discomfort is not often openly expressed, particularly in "liberal" settings. Rather it is felt in the questions that are never asked and in the comments that bring silence. There are only so many times I can ask someone how their spouse, children, etc. are doing and never hear the same concerns returned. I've come to expect this "quiet condemnation" in some situations, but to wonder why I accept it in others. It seems easier to avoid those situations that are optional rather than to try to change them (admittedly not the best attitude).
>
> The April 1992 draft of "Procedures for Marriage . . . " amplifies these feelings. I and others have put much effort into many forums and other more personal efforts designed to address the issue of same-sex marriage. The sum total of these efforts is relegated to "Durham Friends recognize that such a relationship [as marriage] may be sought by many sorts of couples—young and old, heterosexual and homosexual, . . . " While a true statement, it says nothing of Meeting's deliberations or decisions

regarding the matter. If same-sex marriage presents no problems and will be treated in the same manner as a heterosexual union, surely this can be directly stated. If there are concerns, they should be mentioned. If certain issues (a few of which I address below) have been visited, they bear comment. It seems to me that this document leaves the issue in a framework of "if a lesbian or gay couple wants to get married, they should apply—then we'll *really* consider it." No couple should be subjected to such an ordeal.

While I'm on my "soapbox," I'm going to address three concerns with same-sex marriage that I've heard expressed by members of meeting. These are not, of course, unique to Durham Friends Meeting. I address them in order from (as I see it) least important to most aggravating.

Legal Concerns: The comment is often, "but same-sex marriage is illegal [unlawful]." As a matter of Friends' tradition and my personal faith, the question of legality should have no bearing whatsoever on Friends' marriage practices. Indeed, many early Friends' marriages were not recognized by the state. Yet meeting must define its position on same-sex marriage with the understanding that it may someday be called to explain and/or defend that position, particularly in a legal framework. Gay men and lesbians are working to change the legal system. A couple married by Durham Meeting may very well use that marriage as a foundation for a challenge of current law.

Biblical Concerns: Dr. Dale Martin and others are able to challenge the notion that homosexuality is prohibited by the Bible on a theological basis. I have a more basic concern with the notion of biblical authority. When I joined meeting, I was never asked about my belief in Christ or in the authority of the Bible. Had I been, I would have answered truthfully that I was not (and am not) a Christian by anyone's standards, including the more lax ones often heard in unprogrammed meetings. I can best describe myself as a universalist. If meeting is now adhering to a biblical writ, I'm anxious to hear the extent of it. In a more sarcastic vein: are we now applying weight standards so as to shun gluttons?

"We'll become a gay-lesbian meeting": This concern is most often expressed in a roundabout way. I recall one member wondering whether a public announcement of meeting's willingness to marry lesbian and gay couples would result in "a lot of requests from new gay and lesbian members." This kind of comment is blatant homophobia. My first response to such is "So what?" A more studied response is "Great! Isn't that what we want?" Lesbians and gay men are either "just folks" or they aren't. There is no middle ground.

Our public comment about our beliefs is our testimony to the world.

I can't imagine that same member feeling comfortable thinking about, let alone suggesting, a policy of being quiet about our peace testimony for fear that "if there's a war, a lot of pacifists will suddenly want to join us." What's worse, members of meeting seem quite willing to hear a homophobic comment without pointing out its essence. In my experience, a statement as equally racist or sexist brings quite a different level of response.[2]

The Ministry and Counsel Committee wrote Jim back to say that "you would be surprised how close in spirit your note is to the feelings of many in meeting." The committee members agreed that it was probably best to get the issue of same-sex marriage resolved. They set up a timetable of six monthly discussion groups, which were to produce a new draft of the marriage procedures. The new draft would then be presented during a meeting for business, at which the matter would be decided. The committee members also mentioned that they had missed Jim during his absence. They were glad to have him back and concerned with what the meeting was doing.

The six discussion sessions were designed to help people air their feelings about same-sex marriage and also to help them think about it in new ways. They began by asking the question of just what "marriage" means to Quakers—Monogamy? Children? Commitment? Growth? Having answered that, the meeting could then talk faithfully about whether or not a same-sex couple could meet those criteria.

The Quaker process is less a matter of two sides trying to persuade each other than, as the Quakers put it, "Friends struggling together to find the truth." Understanding the process by which they do this is the key to understanding the Society of Friends. For it is this struggle to find the truth, rather than any particular dogma, that is at the heart of their religion. Quakers *value* the fact that they disagree on many important issues. John Hunter explains, "Quakers are primarily about process, not about outcome. This Society of Friends can be joined freely and left freely. But we choose to stay and struggle with each other."

For the six meetings on the marriage document, members gathered in the meeting house and formed a circle of chairs. Small children played with toys in the center while the adults talked about their feelings, responding to each other but never really arguing specific points. Yet slowly, over several months, a sense began to form in the meeting that they were finding common ground, that they understood one another's concerns and were closing in on a common truth.

The experience of Cornelia Sparks, an older attender of Durham Friends Meeting, provides a good example of how the process works. She had moved to Durham several months before from Wilton, Connecticut. Her meeting in Wilton had also been discussing the issue of same-sex marriage: two women, one of whom had been raised in the meeting, had asked to be married under its care. That meeting had decided against performing the wedding, and the two women were eventually married under the care of another Quaker meeting. Cornelia had been unable to attend any of the Wilton meeting's discussions on the subject, however, because she had been nursing her husband through the final stages of terminal cancer.

Cornelia had some serious reservations about the idea of same-sex marriage. In one of the early discussions, she talked about her fear of the legal repercussions of performing a gay marriage; she thought it was all too possible that the state of North Carolina might retaliate by revoking the right of Quakers to perform any marriages. Cornelia talked about Quaker history, about the early years when the Church of England, and hence the government of England, had refused to recognize marriages performed by Quaker meetings. For years, couples had gone from meeting to meeting, gathering more and more signatures witnessing their marriage document, until finally the government had agreed to recognize them. After such a long struggle to have their marriages approved by the state in the first place, did Quakers really want to risk losing it all by marrying gay and lesbian couples?

After Cornelia's words, the meeting sat in silence for a while, reflecting on what she had said. Later in the evening, another member was moved to talk about what he thought was important about Quaker history. Friends had a tradition, he said, of thinking first about what was right, and then worrying about what was legal. Friends had helped run the underground railroad because they had decided that slavery was wrong, even if helping a slave to escape was illegal. Friends had given sanctuary to illegal aliens who were denied asylum because the U.S. government happened to be supporting the dictators that they were fleeing from. And Friends had refused to take up arms, even when drafted, because of their belief that there is that of God in everyone, that to do violence to another human being is an act against God. Quakers had traditionally acted on their own sense of what is right, and stood up to fight the law when it contradicted that.

At a later meeting, Cornelia talked about more basic feelings that she had. She could understand a same-sex couple wanting to have a ceremony. "I can certainly understand the desire of a couple who wish to commit to one another on a lifetime basis, to have a celebration, an exchanging of promises or vows, a certificate that they can look to for the rest of their lives. You know, I have my wedding document hanging in my den, even though I'm a widow. To me, that's a very important part of my life." But Cornelia also said that she was very uncomfortable with calling such a gay or lesbian relationship a marriage. On some basic level, she believed that marriage had to be between a man and a woman.

After a period of silence to reflect on Cornelia's feelings, another Friend admitted that she had once felt much the same way. But the more that she explored what marriage really meant to her, the more she realized that a gay or lesbian couple could be "married" in the way that she understood the word to mean. For example, her first thought had been, "Well, marriage is all about raising a family, and gays can't have children, so why do they need to get married?" But then she asked herself if she would be comfortable marrying a man and a woman who were too old to have children. She was forced to admit that she would. And the more she asked herself questions like that, the more she realized that her discomfort with gay and lesbian marriages was simply fear of something that she wasn't accustomed to, rather than any Spirit-led objection. Having realized that it was just fear, she was prepared to confront it.

Later in that meeting, another Friend broke the silence to talk about how uncomfortable she would feel if the meeting decided to use the term "marriage" for straight couples and "celebration" for gay couples. It was too much like the old days of segregation, when there were separate water fountains for "whites" and "coloreds." Yes, "marriage" has a very sacred and special meaning. So what are we saying to the gay and lesbian members of meeting if we forbid them to use that word? That their relationships are not as sacred or special as straight ones? That they are not as loving or committed? That they are somehow less deserving of that word? She talked about the gay and lesbian members of meeting that she knew and respected, and how hurtful and wrong she thought it would be to tell them that their love was not as good as straight love.

Before the meeting ended, Cornelia spoke again, to remind them that she had only been honest about the way she really felt. Although she was uncomfortable using the word "marriage" for same-sex unions, she could also understand why some people would think it important to use that very word. If the meeting decided that it wanted to take a gay or lesbian marriage under its care, then she would not stand in the way of it. She would be willing to stand aside in such a case.

A month later, at the next discussion session, Cornelia broke the silence to say that she had been exploring her feelings about the word "marriage" and what it really meant to her. She had decided that if a same-sex couple were truly in love, then the word could apply to them. Rather than standing aside, she would stand with the meeting if it decided to celebrate such a wedding.

By the end of the six-month discussion period, it was obvious that most of the meeting had arrived at clearness on the issue. Attendance at the last two forums, which had been reserved for unresolved problems, dropped off dramatically, indicating that most members felt that there were no problems left to resolve. Jim Gilkeson recalls, "People have told us, 'Well, it's starting to get old. I mean, I'm pretty much clear on this, and I'm supportive of this, and I'm not quite sure why we're still having forum after forum after forum.' "

A majority is not enough, however, in the Quaker process. Even one member with a heartfelt objection can prevent a meeting from moving forward on an issue. And at Durham Friends Meeting, there was one such member.

When Don Markle had first learned that Durham Friends Meeting was thinking about performing gay and lesbian marriages, he immediately wrote a letter to the Ministry and Counsel Committee. In it he outlined his belief that homosexuality is a sin, and that by condoning a homosexual marriage the meeting would create a "stumbling block to a homosexual coming into a personal relationship with God".[3] In adherence to Quaker tradition, Don had been invited to serve on the marriage document committee, to help the group struggle to find the truth. While the rest of the meeting gradually came to clearness on their willingess to celebrate same-sex marriages, however, Don remained adamantly opposed to them. None of the forums did anything to change Don's mind. At every turn, Don stated his basic objection: the Bible says that homosexuality is wrong.

Both in the forums and outside them, various Friends tried to talk with Don about his feelings. Why did he think homosexuality is wrong? Who did he think was hurt by it? What danger did it represent? Don argued that male homosexuality was dangerous because it exposed the participants to AIDS, and that by condoning homosexuality the meeting would be promoting the spread of that disease. But from Don's point of view, such objections were secondary. What really mattered was the Bible's condemnation of homosexuality. "In Christian ethics," he says, "you're either doing what God says, or you're doing what you believe ought to be right. And doing the latter, you'll eventually be captured by the evil one on his side. So you've got to accept what God says."

Friends talked to Don about his belief that the Bible is infallible. They argued that while there was that of God within those who wrote the Bible, they were still only mortal men, and may have unwittingly endorsed some of their society's preconceptions without questioning them. How else could one explain why Paul, who condemns homosexuals, also wrote in support of slavery as a moral institution?

None of this, however, shook Don's belief that the Bible was perfectly right. As he saw it, "If the main mission of people on earth is to come into relationships with God through Christ, then slavery is probably irrelevant. In fact, we screwed up if slavery was endorsed by God. If we had treated those people as Christians ought to be treated, as master to a slave and a slave to a master, it would have been fine. It would have been like family.

"Slavery could have been a wonderful institution. There are a lot of people who don't want the responsibility. It could have been a wonderful situation. Kind of the way that families are. I mean, kids are slaves to their parents. But most people would like to stay in those relationships." (He later explained that he was not, however, advocating a system of *racial* slavery.)[4]

Other Friends were more willing to accept Don's belief in an inerrant Bible, but questioned what some of the passages really meant. As they saw it, if you go back to the original Greek in which the New Testament was written, some of these passages seem to mean entirely different things. Again, Don found such arguments to be irrelevant: "In order to believe that, you have to have faith in other information that has come along. People try to tell you, 'Well, you have to realize what it was like at the time.

The situation at the time according to scholars was this.'—So you have to have faith in the scholars. And in my mind, and in what the Bible says, the wisdom of man is nothing compared to the wisdom of God. In my mind, God is an active God, and he would protect the Bible and the interpretations as it came through, if this is going to be his guiding light."

One of the principal tenets of the Quaker faith is the notion of Continuing Revelation. This means that the truth can never be fully known and captured in some set of written laws, that we continuously learn new things that were unknown to our ancestors, that each generation finds new parts of the truth and slowly gets a better understanding of it by struggling to understand one another. Jim Gilkeson explains, "A true Quaker would believe that we have a better understanding of morality and ethics now than people did when the Bible was written. Not to say that we all follow it better. Not that everyone has it. But sort of as a unit, the human race has a better understanding now than it did then, simply because more time has passed. Over time we do come to understand things better."

Continuing Revelation means that Quakers must be open to new and unexpected truths. Although Don said repeatedly that he upheld the notion, his statements indicated otherwise. In fact, Don seemed to believe that an open mind is an open door to damnation.

"The intellectual realm is dangerous. One of the reasons that Satan fell from heaven is pride, and intellectual pride at having a better idea than God. That's why Satan's out and the battle is going on. And he's going to use that in every way that he can for that evil force.

"One of the things that is necessary for me is that God doesn't change his mind. Because if he changes his mind he could change his mind about salvation as well. And the way the Bible is constructed, he can't change his mind."

Don represented a real challenge to the Society of Friends. As a group, they strive for diversity, welcoming people who may be disruptive to them, people who can bring a different perception of the truth, so that they can struggle together and perhaps find a greater truth. But that system is predicated on a willingness by all the members to share in the struggle, to keep an open mind, and to listen to one another. Over the course of the discussion on the marriage document, it became increasingly clear that Don Markle didn't believe in that underlying process. Indeed, some of the members began to question why Don had chosen to be with them. Rather than being a Quaker, Don seemed to be a fundamentalist, convinced that there was a single absolute truth and sure that he understood it completely.

Don's criticisms of Durham Friends Meeting were particularly revealing. Although every member has a few complaints about the meeting's direction, Don's disagreements cut to the heart of what it means to be a Quaker. For example, he complained that the meeting lacked a specific creed, a written moral code. Yet for Quakers, that is the whole point. Their commitment is based not on the assertion of a particular dogma, but on a process for uncovering the truth.

Don also believed that the meeting was too diverse. He felt that many good Bible-believing Christians would find it impossible to join the meeting because it was open to too many people with other points of view. For him, inclusiveness without limits was dangerous: "Is diversity killing the meeting? I think that's a question that all the Quakers are dealing with. Do they stand for anything? In their efforts to be inclusive, are they watering themselves down to the point that they don't stand for *anything*?"

Don believed that this diversity was preventing the Quakers from being a "beacon to bring people unto Christ. In reality, the evidence is that the Quaker religion is a dying religion right now. We used to have a lot more Quakers than we do now, and we've had a huge population increase. That's not a good sign."

The number of traditional Quakers (nonprogrammed Friends) in the United States has actually been roughly the same since the time of the Revolutionary War. But most Friends see their denomination's small size as a natural byproduct of their faith—Quakers are more interested in searching for the truth than in searching for new members.

"That's one of the disadvantages of not being a proselytizing religion," comments Gilkeson. "You don't win converts because you're not out to win converts."

How would Durham Friends Meeting deal with Don Markle? Could it successfully integrate his vision of the truth with that of the rest of the meeting, or would the meeting deadlock over the issue? There had been times before when all the members of a meeting couldn't agree on an issue, and there were mechanisms in place to deal with such a situation. John Hunter explains, "There have been many times when a strongly held opinion by one or two has not been changed. In that case, there is a maturity that is demanded of members, and members need to know this coming into meeting. It's an issue of seasoning. The person who has the minority opinion, especially if he or she is just one out of what is clearly a sense of the meeting going the opposite direction, has to make an *awfully* difficult decision: to really look within themselves to know if their issue and the way they're holding it is really important and spiritually led. Then they have the obligation of sticking by their guns. Or if they can see that the sense of the meeting is going somewhere, and these other people are equally Spirit-led and seeing it differently, then they can make the decision to stand aside. And maybe register a dissenting opinion, but stand aside. Because the caring for the meeting is greater than is the particular issue. And realizing that Quakers are primarily about process, not about outcome."

Several Friends spoke with Don to make sure that he understood the concept of "standing aside." Don, however, did not feel that he could stand aside in good conscience. As Don saw it, if he stood aside, Durham Friends Meeting would one day marry a gay or lesbian couple. That would send an unacceptable message to the gay community, that their lifestyle was respectable, and Don would have personally condoned it with his silence.

"What would be the interpretation from outside the meeting?" he asked. "Say I'm in the homosexual community, and I'm looking for acceptance, and I want people not to harass me, and I want to be treated the same way heterosexuals are. Then I would see that I've now got somebody on my side, someone who's endorsed it. The homosexuals will say, 'Well, the meeting accepted it, why can't you accept it?' to the Baptists or someone else."

It was entirely possible for Don to prevent the meeting from ever marrying a gay or lesbian couple during his lifetime. Although there are provisions for dealing with a lone holdout, they are almost never used. John Hunter explains, "In the older days, people were read out of meeting. They were removed from membership and the problem was solved that way. That has not been done, to my knowledge, in our branch of Friends in modern times. That is so extreme, and such an admission of failure of the process." Even Gilkeson, who disagreed with Don's stand, was hesitant about such a move. "I'm not sure it's a step that even I would want to see happen."

Thus the issue seemed to be stalemated. But even a stalemate has consequences. One gay man who'd been attending the meeting for about a year said that he wouldn't apply for full membership until the issue was resolved. As he put it, he wanted to know what membership in the meeting meant before he requested it.

Jim, too, felt a deep need to get the issue resolved. "If business meeting is unable or unwilling to do this, I would have to consider laying down my membership in Durham Meeting. Possibly consider joining Chapel Hill Meeting. At some point it becomes a matter of conscience, a matter of faith. To be a part of a spiritual community, I have to feel like that spiritual community sees me as a full part of it, and accepts me. If they can't do that, then I have no place here."

On November 14, 1993, Durham Friends Meeting gathered for their monthly meeting for worship with attention to business. It was the best-attended meeting that anyone could remember. It was also the longest meeting that anyone could recall.

The clerk of meeting read a letter from Don Markle, in which he resigned his membership. It was a long letter, citing a number of biblical passages, but it basically said that Don felt it was time for him to move on to a community of faith that shared more of his beliefs. That same afternoon, Durham Friends Meeting approved a minute stating that it would consider requests for marriage by gay and lesbian couples on the same footing as requests from straight couples. The minute recognized that there was a diversity of opinion within the meeting on this subject: "Not all of us are comfortable with same gender marriage or the use of the word marriage to describe such a union." Indeed, one member stood aside and asked that his specific concerns be minuted. Still, the meeting had reached clearness on the matter. "It is the sense of the meeting that we move forward with this decision."

Soon thereafter Jim Gilkeson and his lover wrote a letter to the meeting describing their love for each other and how their relationship had helped each of them to grow, and asking to be married under the care of the meeting. A Clearness Committee was formed, with the hope of providing the couple with the benefit of a wide range of experiences. It included a gay father, a lesbian mother, young married people, older married people, as well as people who had been through divorces. The committee met with the couple a number of times. Although they had been together for four years, Jim and his lover still had a lot of unresolved issues to work through: Jim's desire to raise children, their different career paths, their plans for the future. After several months of counseling, the couple came to clearness—but it turned out to be clearness that they should *not* get married.

CHAPTER 9

Race, the Vatican, and Inclusiveness: Holy Cross

"You people are living a flight of fancy to think that the Church will ever change," said Monseignor Michael Swalina.

"To say that the Church will never change is to deny historical reality," responded Kevin Calegari. "In addition, we have hope. Our hope is stronger than your denial. Our faith is stronger than your fear."

—*an exchange in the Congregation for the Doctrine of the Faith, Vatican City, July 25, 1992*

It's not surprising that the congregation of Holy Cross is protective of its role as a black Catholic church. Holy Cross was established in 1938 by Jesuit missionaries as a church for blacks in Durham. Because the Jesuits are an independent order, Holy Cross did not fall under the control of the local bishop. It was a fact that saved the church's life.

During the 1950s Bishop Waters had, in a well-intentioned move, decided to integrate his congregations. At the time it was a gutsy decision. Only a few years before, his decision to integrate the Catholic schools had sparked violent protests, demonstrations by the Ku Klux Klan, and even several acts of sabotage against church property. Still, the bishop felt that this was the right thing to do. By integrating its congregations, the church would help to tear down the barriers between the races and build a more united faith. Blacks and whites who prayed together were sure to get along better.

In practice, however, integration meant that black churches were simply closed down and their congregations told to begin attending the nearest white church. The sense of community that had built up around the black churches was destroyed, and blacks who had been leaders in their own churches found themselves starting over again as newcomers in the white churches. Integration meant that blacks had to fit into the white community, not vice versa.

Holy Cross survived because it was a Jesuit mission and was therefore not subject to the bishop's orders. However, that independence would itself bring about other challenges to its existence. Over the years, Holy Cross would get caught in the tug of war between the bishop and the Jesuits. At one point the bishop even made plans to open a second black church in Durham so that he could close down Holy Cross and transfer its members to a church under his control. The plan was eventually blocked by heavy lobbying on the part of Holy Cross's leadership. Still, history has given the congregation reason to be defensive of Holy Cross and its special position in the black community.

In 1969 a series of classified ads began running in a Los Angeles newspaper. The ads announced the formation of Dignity, a group for gay and lesbian Roman Catholics, and gave contact numbers for those who would like to attend a meeting. The initial group had fewer than twenty members. By the end of 1971, however, the group had grown to 158 dues-paying members. By the end of 1992, that number would reach 4,000.

In the early 1970s, Dignity enjoyed the support of many members of the Catholic clergy. A number of priests and many bishops as well were sympathetic to the growing gay civil rights movement. When a new Dignity chapter formed to serve Raleigh and Durham, it did so with the blessing of the new bishop. In fact, Bishop Gossman said mass for the group on several occasions.

For many members of Dignity, celebrating mass is the most important thing they do together. The new Raleigh-Durham chapter arranged for mass to be said by several different local priests, on a rotating basis. Because the chapter had no home church, it rotated meeting places as well—sometimes at the cathedral in Raleigh, sometimes at St. Michael's in Cary, sometimes at Holy Cross in Durham, sometimes in the home of a member.

At first the new chapter advertised its meetings in the *North Carolina Catholic*. There was a strong conservative response to the ads, however, and Bishop Gossman received phone calls from parishioners who were outraged at seeing such an ad in their paper. Gossman asked the local chapter of Dignity to cease advertising in Roman Catholic publications.

The restriction made it difficult for Dignity to reach the people who most needed to hear about the new organization—other gay and lesbian Catholics. But one does not turn down a request from the bishop, and the local chapter reluctantly agreed to it.

When Janet Jezsik first arrived in Durham in 1984, she shopped around for a church. She never felt drawn to any of them, however, until she happened to try a little black church near the campus of North Carolina Central University.

As a white woman, Janet felt a little out of place at Holy Cross. But she found herself drawn in by the sense of community at the place. This wasn't a big, impersonal church. It was more like family.

"I was used to a church where we said things like, 'Well, we pray for world peace.' These people were saying, 'My mother is sick, and she's in Louisiana, and we're going to all go over there. So we're asking for your prayers for her and for our trip. We expect to be back in town a week from today.' "

Janet was progressive and had always supported the civil rights movement. Still, being in the minority was a new experience for her. For once, Janet didn't automatically fit in. But she gradually got to know the people in the congregation, and she came to understand how the church worked. "There are about fifteen families that are the heart and soul of that church," she says. Over the next year and a half, as those families got to know her, they began asking her about her background, talking with her after mass, and having her over to dinner. Slowly Janet began to feel accepted in her new church.

Janet knew that there were limits on the roles that she could hope to play at Holy Cross. Although about 30 percent of the congregation is now white, the church is still chartered as a black church, and the leadership positions are effectively reserved for blacks. "It was real clear to me," says Janet. "I understood that I would never have a primary leadership role in the church." Still, there were many committees that she could serve on and many ways for her to be an active member of the parish. It was a wonderful church, and Janet had found a home where she could pray.

In 1985, a new priest came to Holy Cross. Like his predecessor, Father Bruce Bavinger supported the local chapter of Dignity. He said mass for them every six weeks or so, and allowed them to continue using Holy Cross as one of their meeting sites.

Vatican City. In 1986 the Congregation for the Doctrine of the Faith (CDF) released a document titled "A Letter to the Bishops of the Catholic Church on the Pastoral Care of Homosexual Persons." The letter was approved by Pope John Paul II and was signed by Cardinal Ratzinger, prefect of the Congregation for the Doctrine of the Faith. The letter read in part: "As in every moral disorder, homosexual activity prevents one's own fulfillment and happiness by acting contrary to the wisdom of God. The Church, in rejecting erroneous opinions regarding homosexuality, does not limit but rather defends personal freedom and dignity as realistically understood."

The letter expressed the CDF's concern that many Roman Catholic bishops, particularly in the United States, seemed to be supporting basic civil rights for homosexuals such as freedom from discrimination in housing or employment. "There is an effort in some countries to manipulate the Church by gaining the often well-intentioned support of her pastors, with a view to changing civil statutes and laws."

The CDF instructed Catholic bishops to oppose any form of civil rights protection for homosexuals. It explained that homosexuality was an inherent evil and a threat to the traditional place of the family in society. Although the CDF did recognize the essential humanity of homosexuals and found the violence being done to them "deplorable," it also implied that gays had brought such violence on themselves. As the CDF saw it, it was the gay community's attempt to gain basic civil rights that had brought about antigay violence: "When civil legislation is introduced to protect behavior to which no one has any conceivable right, neither the Church nor society should be surprised when other distorted notions and practices gain ground, and irrational and violent reactions increase."

The CDF also singled out Dignity as a particularly dangerous organization that needed to be supressed.

> . . . increasing numbers of people today, even within the Church, are bringing enormous pressure to bear on the Church to accept the homosexual condition as though it were not disordered and to condone homosexual activity. . . . The Church's ministers must ensure that homosexual persons in their care will not be misled by this point of view, so pro-

foundly opposed to the teaching of the Church. But the risk is great, and there are many who seek to create confusion regarding the Church's position and then to use that confusion to their own advantage. . . . No authentic pastoral program will include organizations in which homosexual persons associate with each other without clearly stating that homosexual activity is immoral."

. . . Special attention should be given to the practice of scheduling religious services and to the use of Church buildings by these groups, including the facilities of Catholic schools and colleges. To some, such permission to use Church property may seem only just and charitable: but in reality it is contradictory to the purpose for which these institutions were founded, it is misleading and often scandalous.[1]

The Congregation for the Doctrine of the Faith was established in the year 1233. Until 1965, however, it was known as the Holy and Roman Inquisition.

Dignity USA responded to the CDF letter quickly, calling it "cruel and unChristian." "We believe that lesbian and gay Catholics are numbered among the people of God, and that they can express their sexuality in a manner that is responsible, loving, and consonant with Christ's message."[2]

Prior to the Ratzinger letter, relations between Dignity and the Roman Catholic church had been unclear. Many bishops had supported the organization; many others had not. The CDF letter, however, served as a declaration of war between the Vatican and Dignity. Prior to 1986, virtually all of Dignity's chapters had been meeting in Catholic churches, with the support of their priests. By 1992, only three or four chapters across the country could still do so. The exact number is difficult to verify, because those that do remain in the church must keep a low profile.

In Durham, the Ratzinger letter had an immediate and chilling impact on the relationship between the local chapter of Dignity and Bishop Gossman. Thomas Sherratt, a member of the chapter at the time, explains, "After the Ratzinger letter it was no longer possible for any bishop, if he valued his job, to be gay-accepting. The bishop's approach since the Ratzinger letter has been one of benign neglect— 'If I don't know about it, then I don't have to deal with it, and what my priests may choose to do with it is their business.' "

In spite of the CDF letter, though, a number of local priests, including

Father Bavinger, were still willing to say mass for the group. Dignity continued holding services, rotating the location every week.

By 1987, however, it was clear that this arrangement wasn't working. There was perpetual confusion among the members about where to go each week, and it was very hard for other gay Catholics to find the group or get in contact with it. Several members of Dignity approached Father Bavinger and asked if the group could begin holding all of its services at Holy Cross. After they had explained the reason for the request, Bavinger agreed to it.

Janet had always believed that she held to something she referred to as the "black agenda." For her that meant working on issues of class— poverty, hunger, and teen pregnancy. Many African-Americans, however, see the "black agenda"—if it exists—as being one of securing civil rights and economic opportunity. It would be grossly unfair to say that the congregation of Holy Cross didn't care about Janet's issues. They saw their principal focus, however, to be one of helping their community by working within the establishment—by gaining access to the political system, getting access to the banking system, and shattering the glass ceiling that hindered their advancement.

There was also a certain degree of class friction between Janet and others in the congregation. The parishioners of Holy Cross were mainly professionals, including a number of well-connected bankers and lawyers, and represented much of the leadership of the black community in Durham. They gave heavily to charity, but they also saw nothing wrong with being successful themselves. Janet, in contrast, tended to be somewhat distrustful of wealth. "I made a conscious decision to live very modestly and very simply," she says. Symbols of conspicuous consumption made her uneasy. "It was hard for me to go to church and see all those BMWs and Saabs in an age when we all knew that there were terrible excesses in the eighties."

After a while, though, Janet came to decide that much of what she was seeing simply reflected a difference in the black and white experience. As a white woman, Janet could dress in very inexpensive clothes and still expect to be treated with a basic amount of respect. It is not an option that is always open to blacks. As she explains, "I would go to church and dress very modestly. But in the black culture it is so important to dress for success every day. That's the black experience—they don't have the option of dressing casually, because they constantly have to be above reproach.

Outside of their three-piece suits, some of these people would probably be stopped by police for jogging in a neighborhood that isn't their own."

In 1989 several members of Holy Cross's Parish Council came to Father Bavinger to ask him about the Dignity group that was using the church on Sunday nights. One of the council members had seen an advertisement for a gay Catholic group in a local paper and had recognized the phone number of Bavinger's office in Holy Cross. Bavinger admitted that he had been answering the phone for the group and giving out information on Dignity to anyone who asked for it. The council members were extremely unhappy to see Holy Cross's name linked with homosexuality in any public way. They told Bavinger to get rid of Dignity— the group was not welcome at Holy Cross.

Bavinger responded firmly to their request: this was a pastoral decision, and the pastor was saying that Dignity would stay. The council grudgingly accepted his decision.

In truth, Bavinger's stand had been pure bravado. He knew that if calls started going to his superiors, eventually someone would order him to expel the group. He told Dignity members that they would have to be more secretive—no more advertisements, and no more giving out his phone number.

In 1990 one of the few Spanish-speaking priests in Durham was transferred away. That left only two bilingual priests in the area, one of whom was Father Bavinger. Several members of the Hispanic community approached Bavinger and asked if he would be willing to hold a Spanish-language mass for them. Bavinger agreed, and thereafter scheduled Spanish-language masses once a month at Holy Cross, on Sunday afternoons. The monthly masses were very popular, and attendance soon rivaled that of his regular Sunday morning services.

Janet had always known that she found other women attractive. It took her a long time, however, to understand that she was a lesbian. When the realization finally hit, her first concern was how this would affect her relationship with her church: "I remember it was absolutely vital for me to tell my pastor what I now knew about myself. Because my worst-case scenario

was being shunned by the church. So much of my heritage and so much of my traditions were tied up in it.

"Fortunately," she says, "the pastor of my church was not at all judgmental."

Janet was very nervous when she went to her first Dignity meeting in 1990. She had no idea what to expect. But when she got there, she found a friendly group of people performing a traditional vespers service. Very soon, she felt right at home.

At about the same time that Janet joined Dignity, she found herself becoming increasingly disillusioned with Holy Cross. Although she loved many of the people there, she began to realize that there were some issues which, though very important to her, the church would never deal with. "Social justice, things like Central America, things that a progressive white person like myself invests a lot of time in—those issues aren't being addressed."

In particular, Janet was frustrated by the fact that the church would never talk about sexual issues in any way, even when they were life threatening. For example, there was one family in the congregation that was adopting AIDS babies. Knowing that the children would most likely never live to be teenagers, the family still wanted to give them as many happy years as possible. But when it came to talking about how to prevent AIDS, the church was silent. Janet complained, "We never addressed those bedroom issues that lead to AIDS."

Similarly, teen pregnancy was never discussed. When a fire broke out in a chicken-processing plant in Hamlet, North Carolina, and twenty-nine people died, the congregation of Holy Cross raised nearly $10,000 to help the victims' families. But Janet thought it was significant that they never talked about the fact that twenty-five of those twenty-nine workers had been single black mothers. "We never talked about teenage pregnancy. I had to stand through the baptism of a baby born to a single parent. And I personally found it very difficult knowing that this young woman had every advantage to not have a child as a single parent. To me, that's very compromising."

There were other issues as well. As a devoted pacifist, Janet was horrified by the Persian Gulf War. In 1991 Janet organized a mass in protest of the conflict. The U.S. military has been one of the best opportunities for

African-Americans seeking economic and educational advancement, however, and many members of Holy Cross were ardent supporters of the armed forces. When Janet arrived at church the next week, she found that the banner she had made reading "We shall beat our swords into plowshares" had been taken down and replaced with an American flag and a sign reading, "God Bless Our Troops."

After that, Janet says, "I started attending less frequently, because my progressive white agenda certainly includes the black community, but none of my needs as a progressive white person were being met there."

In 1991 Father Bavinger was hospitalized with a serious infection. Although he returned to his duties at Holy Cross, members of the Parish Council began questioning whether he was spreading himself too thin, ministering to too many groups. That led to a discussion of a subject that had been worrying the council for some time—the loss of focus on Holy Cross's black identity.

On April 8, 1992, Father Bavinger asked the Parish Council if he could begin celebrating a second Spanish mass every month. He was expecting a routine approval of the request. The council's reaction caught him by surprise. The Parish Council was highly disturbed by the idea of a second group coming into the church and having a separate mass. It was seen as a possible prelude to a takeover of the church.

"It kind of set off something that had been brewing for a while," says Bavinger, "about people having their own masses, and Holy Cross becoming a place where different groups are looking at their own thing. That does not register well with the black community at all.

"Separate but equal has usually been a situation where the blacks got the short end. So there was a real natural impulse to say, 'No, let's have everybody be one parish, with all the masses open to everybody. Nobody gets their own mass.' That was sparked by the Hispanic issue, but it also included Dignity."

Bavinger worked to reach some compromise with the Parish Council. But instead of being contained, the problem expanded. Bavinger had assumed that Dignity would be left out of the discussion—after all, the group was too small to possibly threaten a takeover of Holy Cross.

"All along, I was hoping that Dignity would not be brought into the conversation. I was hoping that if we could resolve the Hispanic thing,

Dignity would be left alone. But they just kept saying, 'No, no. Dignity too, Dignity too.' "

The Parish Council set about drafting a "Statement of Inclusiveness," which would forbid any group at Holy Cross from holding a mass separate from the main congregation. This would have the effect of canceling both the Hispanic services and Dignity's masses.

Vatican City. On June 25, 1992, the Congregation for the Doctrine of the Faith sent another letter to Roman Catholic bishops, this one entitled, "Some Considerations Concerning the Catholic Response to Legislative Proposals on the Non-Discrimination of Homosexual Persons." Although the CDF did not publicly identify the author, Monsignor Michael Swalina admitted that much of it had been drafted by Catholic priests in the United States—principally members of the Colorado church hierarchy who wanted Vatican support for a statewide repeal of local gay and lesbian nondiscrimination ordinances. One of the principal authors is believed to have been Archbishop Francis Stafford of Denver.

"Recently," read the letter, "legislation has been proposed in various places which would make discrimination on the basis of sexual orientation illegal. . . . Such initiatives, even when they seem more directed toward support of basic civil rights than condonement of homosexual activity or homosexual lifestyle, may in fact have a negative impact on the family and society."

The letter called on Catholics to oppose any sort of basic civil rights for homosexuals and to support repeal of any nondiscrimination laws which protected them. To support its position, the CDF raised the old stereotype of gays as child molesters and weaklings: "There are areas in which it is not unjust discrimination to take sexual orientation into account, for example, in the placement of children for foster care, in employment of teachers or athletic coaches, and in military recruitment." It was a statement that conveniently overlooked the actual statistics on child molestation, most of which, as noted earlier, is perpetrated by straight men against young girls.

Similarly, the CDF chose to overlook the fact that homosexuality is no longer considered a mental disorder, at least not by mainstream organizations such as the American Psychiatric Association. Instead, the CDF argued that homosexuals are mentally deranged, and thus society has a responsibility to limit their rights: "Thus, it is accepted that the state may restrict the exercise of rights, for example, in the case of contagious or mentally ill persons, in order to protect the common good."[3]

As with the 1986 document, this letter would have a chilling effect on relations between Dignity and the Catholic clergy. It was now even more difficult for any priest or bishop to support the group openly, or to take any stand in favor of the basic civil rights of gay and lesbian persons.

Eight days before the Parish Council meeting at which the inclusion statement would be voted on, Janet attended a Tuesday night mass. Afterward she went over to Father Bavinger to ask how he was doing. He said that he was feeling fine, and that just for her information, it looked like the Parish Council would be voting on a "Statement of Inclusiveness" at their meeting next week. When he saw that this didn't mean anything to Janet, he explained further.

"It means that every mass would have to be open to every member of the church."

Janet still didn't get it.

"It means," said Father Bavinger, "that Dignity wouldn't be able to celebrate mass here anymore."

Janet was stunned. She couldn't believe that something like this could be happening, and no one had even told them about it. She was even more surprised when Father Bavinger asked her to keep the information to herself.

"I have no choice," she said. "I have to talk to the rest of Dignity about this."

At Dignity's next Sunday evening mass, she broke the news to the rest of the group. After some discussion, they phoned Father Bavinger to ask if they could at least send someone to speak at the meeting, to represent their point of view. Bavinger agreed to get them on the meeting's agenda.

The group decided that they should send two representatives who were members of both Dignity and Holy Cross. Paul Illecki would be one, Janet Jezsik would be the other.

It struck me when I interviewed Durham Dignity members that this particular chapter is all white. I asked Bavinger if this might have contributed to tensions with Holy Cross. He said no, for the simple reason that no one in the church knew Dignity well enough to realize that there were no black members or, for that matter, who any of the members were at all. He continued, "Most people didn't even know that Dignity was meeting there. They kept a real low profile, and that was pretty much by design for the past five or six years. Because even though the bishop wasn't going to bother Dignity, if you have a lot of people writing in or writing over his head to somebody else and saying, 'What are you going to do about this? This is not in keeping with Church law!' then Gossman would have to do something."

On July 8, the Parish Council met to vote on the new "Statement of Inclusiveness." Members of the Hispanic community had come to speak, as well as Janet and Paul.

"We felt confident that we could impact the decision," says Janet. After all, Janet had been a member of the parish for years. She'd shared meals with these people. They didn't know her as a lesbian, but they knew her as a person. She'd taught many of the eight-week candidates' courses for new converts to Catholicism, and a number of her students were in the room. And although Paul had only been at Holy Cross for about a year, he was in the choir, which made him visible and fairly well known in the congregation.

Yet they were both surprised by the feelings of the people there. The tone of the meeting seemed formal to the point of hostility. "You will address all your remarks to me," said the president of the Parish Council. "Be aware that all your remarks are being tape-recorded." Janet looked at him in disbelief. This was a man who had converted to Catholicism three years earlier, and she had been the one who had taught his candidates' class.

"There was a very adversarial set to the the whole thing," she remembers. "When I started, I kept looking at people, and I thought, 'It's *me*! You know me!' But I couldn't get through to them. And as I spoke, I knew in my heart that it was over."

When Janet spoke, she was coming out to most of the people in that room. "Hello. I'm Janet Jezsik. I've been a member of your parish for eight years, and I'm also a Catholic lesbian woman."

Janet talked about what Dignity was, about its small contributions to the financial health of Holy Cross over the years, and about how little of Father Bavinger's time the group actually used. She explained that Dignity was purely a community of faith. "We have never used church property or space for political endeavors. Our lives are very political, but we gather here for only one reason. And that is to pray."

Janet tried to help the Parish Council understand why Dignity was so important to her. "I consider myself a member of Holy Cross, but I also consider myself a member of Dignity, and I need both of those. I need to worship with the Holy Cross community, but obviously I've never acknowledged that I was gay to the larger community, never celebrated that part of my life, never could. Dignity fills in the blanks. There I am worshiping as a Catholic who is gay."

Paul spoke after Janet. Since Paul had once been a priest, some of the council members were particularly surprised to learn that he was gay. Paul spoke very simply from his own experience, of a time when he found himself attending a wedding mass and realized that there was nothing in that ceremony that reflected his life. He too needed Holy Cross, but he also needed Dignity. He needed something that celebrated the quality of *his* life, and not just that of the straight majority.

After Janet and Paul spoke, Father Bavinger asked them both to leave so that the council could discuss the matter. In the very brief debate that followed, not one council member discussed the morality or immorality of homosexual behavior. But at the end of the meeting, all fifteen members of the council voted unanimously to adopt the Statement of Inclusiveness, which effectively forbade gay or Spanish-language masses.

That same evening, however, the Parish Council worked out a special arrangement with the Hispanic community. Although Father Bavinger would not be allowed to hold his monthly Spanish mass, he would be allowed to perform a weekly bilingual mass, in which he would alternate between English and Spanish. Although the idea was to make these Sunday afternoon masses more accessible to the English-speaking members of Holy Cross, few of them attended. For all practical purposes, the bilingual service remains a separate mass for the Hispanic community.

No similar arrangement was ever suggested for Dignity. Father Bavinger explained, "It's kind of awkward. There is some fear about what you're saying yes to. Even to say 'Dignity, we want you here, but not with your own mass. We want you to worship with us together.' Even there, we're wondering, 'What are we really saying? Do we want to have same-sex couples holding hands and kissing during services?' "

Whatever the arguments for or against the "Statement of Inclusiveness," the end result was clear. The Hispanic community was welcomed because it was not gay, and Dignity was expelled because it was.

It is in many ways a supremely ironic situation: the Parish Council was keenly aware of the need for a black church, a place where blacks could gather as a community and pray. Yet they were unable to understand why homosexuals would want exactly the same thing—a chance to meet together in their own community of faith.

Janet received the phone call around 10:30 that night. It was a woman from the Parish Council, who clearly felt awkward about being the one to deliver the bad news. She ended the call by saying, "I'll pray for you."

"No," said Janet, "I'll pray for you."

Three years earlier, Bavinger had stepped in to save Dignity. This time he would not. When interviewed, he said that the reasons for expelling Dignity were altogether different this time around.

"Throwing Dignity out because they were homosexual was not where I'm at, and I don't think it's where the diocese is at. As far as the issue goes, I really became convinced that it wasn't homophobia, primarily anyway, but a sense of the black experience. When things get divided up, there is a constant little fear, sometimes a great fear, that Holy Cross would be shut down as a black parish."

The political situation was also substantially different for Bavinger than it had been three years ago. It was one thing to refuse a request from three council members in 1989; it was quite another to disregard a resolution that had been passed unanimously by all fifteen of them. There was also the matter of the latest letter from the CDF. If he opposed the council, they would just go over his head. And clearly his superiors could not afford to back him up. The Vatican had stated that it didn't want homosexuals meeting in its churches. Regardless of how Bavinger felt about that decision, the Vatican had the power to enforce its will.

Members of Dignity met with Bishop Gossman to protest the Parish Council's decision. Like Bavinger, however, he was in no position to reverse it.

Dignity met at Holy Cross one last time the next Sunday. The group had been given until August to leave, but they decided that there were too many bad feelings for them to stay any longer. The church wanted the keys back, so they turned them in.

"That's how things ended," says Janet. "My pastor never called me, which to this day I just find so personally difficult."

The Vatican finally released a public draft of the CDF's letter on July 23, 1992. At the time, Kevin Calegari was vacationing in Italy. As the president of Dignity USA, Kevin felt that an appropriate response was demanded.

On July 29, he entered the Vatican City carrying a hammer and a nail. Kevin walked up to the office of the Congregation for the Doctrine of the Faith and nailed a large envelope to its doors, marked "Return to sender, Cardinal Ratzinger." In addition to the CDF's latest letter, he enclosed a copy of the New Testament, telling reporters, "I'm sure they can use a copy, since they've obviously never read it."

The incident was widely covered in the Italian press. At least one paper drew the parallel to another religious dissident who had nailed a list of complaints to a cathedral door in Wittenberg in 1517. The headline ran, "Gays Follow in Footsteps of Luther."

After leaving Holy Cross, Dignity met in members' houses for the next several weeks. There were still a number of priests willing to defy the CDF's second letter, so they were able to continue celebrating mass.

Eventually, the group was offered meeting space by St. John's, the Episcopal monastery in Durham. This arrangement lasted for several months, until the monastery was closed down owing to a shortage of manpower and the brothers returned to their mother house in Cambridge, Massachusetts.

Since then, the group has found no stable place to meet. Dignity's membership in Durham has fallen precipitously, and the chapter seems on the verge of extinction.

Shortly after Dignity left Holy Cross, David Kirkpatrick was appointed to the Parish Council. David felt that there had been a great deal of misunderstanding between Dignity and the council. He set up a series of lunches at which members of both groups could sit down and talk and at least try to understand each other.

After two such lunches, however, Janet and Paul gave up. The meetings were very polite, but they weren't accomplishing anything. The core of the church leadership never turned up for them. Each time, they would agree to come. But when the afternoon of the luncheon finally arrived, someone else would always turn up with an excuse for them.

"The heart of the Parish Council has never shown up," says Janet. "They keep saying they will, but when you get there they say, 'Oh, I'm sorry, they couldn't make it.' "

I asked several members of Dignity why, given the Vatican's opposition to even the most basic civil rights for gay men and lesbians, they choose to remain in the Roman Catholic church rather than converting to a more accepting denomination.

Thomas Sherratt explained it this way: "I think there are basically two ways to view the Catholic church. One is to look at the letter of the law of the church, which to my mind is ignorant and destructive. The other way is to look at the individuals in the church, and to realize that those individuals are in fact the church. I have personally experienced profoundly knowledgeable, compassionate, and politically powerful people in the church—priests, nuns, monks, not to mention a multitude of lay people, who have made my path as a gay man in the world immeasurably easier.

"The reason I stay in the Catholic church is because of its tradition of prayer and sacrament. I ultimately came to the Catholic church because of its emphasis on how prayer deepens one's experience of the world. I don't find that in other Christian traditions, except perhaps in Quakerism. And although the Quakers have a fine tradition of prayer, they don't have a tradition of sacrament. Sacrament is an affirmation of the sacredness of the world. It serves as a focusing device that allows me to deepen my experience of the presence of God, and to do that in community.

"The teaching of the Church is only useful insofar as it works. I believe that the Catholic church's teaching on human sexuality—well, quite frankly I think that it's nonexistent. The church is essentially teaching that donkeys fly. And if you teach that donkeys fly, then arguably you don't have a teaching.

"The teaching of the church is not working with gay people, and cannot work until it is radically revised."

Janet Jezsic sees things a little differently. "My sense is that faith is like family. You can distance yourself. You can choose to be noninteractive. You can choose to be very close and engaging and warm and friendly. But nevertheless, they are always your family.

"I have had big fights with the church, and battles of rage, but I also love the church like I love my family. Maybe even more so."

Epilogue

W hat does the future hold? The long-term trend seems to be a greater acceptance of homosexuals in both secular and religious society. It doesn't always appear that way, of course, particularly when you're listening to Jerry Falwell rant about the gay menace or watching a video like the Christian Coalition's *Gay Rights, Special Rights*, or reading about Jesse Helms's latest speech in the Senate. Yet the situation has changed vastly in the past thirty years. The American Psychiatric Association no longer considers homosexuality a disease, and no longer tries to treat it with shock therapy and lobotomies. A person can no longer be arrested for walking into a gay bar. There is now a sizable population of "out" homosexuals who are free to live their lives in a degree of openness and safety that would have shocked their predecessors. An ever-increasing number of Americans have an openly gay or lesbian friend. In polls, a majority of Americans consistently say that a person should not be fired from a job or evicted from his or her apartment just for being gay. And if we still occasionally read about a mother losing custody of her children for being a lesbian, at least such an incident is now considered controversial and newsworthy.

Perhaps most important, Americans are becoming accustomed to seeing gay characters portrayed in the media. In a country whose view of reality is heavily shaped by television, television is increasingly showing viewers that gays and lesbians are their fellow human beings. For the past ten years, there have been an increasing number of gay characters on television and in the movies, and those characters have become less and less like the old stereotypes. Try comparing the gay teenager from the mid-1990s show *My So-Called Life* with the gay window dresser in *Mannequin*, a film from the early 1980s. Or compare the two gay characters on *Roseanne* with the one in *Revenge of the Nerds*. Kids today are growing up seeing gays portrayed as people—flawed people, sometimes even jerks, but still people.

The religious backlash against homosexuals has come about precisely because of the vast sea change that is taking place within American society. Thirty years ago, no one would have bothered going on television to say that homosexuality was sinful. After all, who would have argued with that? Nor would the Vatican have wasted ink writing its bishops to say that homosexuality is immoral. Nor would the Southern Baptist Convention have passed a resolution requiring its member churches to condemn homosexuality. All of these actions have occurred because churches know that the world has changed.

In many ways, the situation is similar to that of the women's rights movement. For all the complaints from conservative religious quarters, for all of Rush Limbaugh's diatribes against "Feminazis," for all the flak that Hillary Clinton gets for having had a higher-paying job than her husband's, the women's movement has basically succeeded. Certainly there are battles left to fight—the glass ceiling in corporate America, the role of women in the armed forces, the ordination of women pastors, and so on. But there has been a fundamental change in how women perceive themselves. Little girls no longer assume that their only job will be that of a wife. College-age women now take it for granted that they can go into virtually any career that they want. And the men of my generation relate to women in a very different way than did the men of my grandfather's.

All of this is not to say that the gay rights movement has yet been as successful as the women's rights movement. As the black civil rights movement showed, progress can come in fast spurts and then slow to a snail's pace for years. But I believe that a greater acceptance of homosexuals is inevitable. As with so many other social changes, the Church will likely remain divided about this issue for some time. Some denominations will be leading the fight to change tradition; others will be fighting just as ferociously to defend it.

Of course, pointing to long-term trends does little to solve immediate conflicts. How can a congregation best handle a dispute over gay and lesbian issues? How can it debate a subject without opening a rift? How can its members struggle with each other while continuing to function as a community of faith?

Giving advice is risky, especially because every church brings its own heritage and experience to controversial questions. Every case is different. It remains my hope that the careful reader will glean useful information from each of the stories in this book and then draw the appropriate conclusions for him- or herself. Nevertheless, I offer the following recommendations to churches that find themselves in conflict over issues involving homosexuality.

1. Be prepared for a generational split. Young people in our society have been exposed to the idea of homosexuality for most of their lives. They've seen it on television, they've talked about it, and they may even have openly gay friends. The idea will never be as completely alien to them as it is to their grandparents.

This means that an older church leader (pastor, council president, deacon) who wants to take a pro-gay stand has an advantage over a younger leader in the same situation. When the old-timers look to see who has raised this disturbing idea, they will find one of their own. If he can think this way about such an issue, then maybe it's not so outrageous. By contrast, a young leader espousing the same views will look like an outsider and an extremist.

2. The best indicator of a pastor's ability to survive a crisis is the length of time he or she has served at the church. I am not saying that a recently appointed minister should run from every conflict. After all, there is more to being a pastor than job security. Still, you should know what chances you're taking before you pick your fights.

I want to stress that this is not a matter of one's experience as a pastor, but of one's experience with a particular congregation. When Jimmy Creech came into conflict with the older members of his church, he had been at Fairmont for only a year. That meant that those who opposed him didn't know him very well— they would form their entire opinion of him based on his handling of this one issue. Similarly, Linda Jordan had been at Binkley for only two years when the conflict over Blevins's licensure began. By contrast, Mahan Siler had been at Pullen for eight years. The congregation already held strong opinions of him before the issue of Kevin and Steven's marriage ever came up. He had prayed with those people, baptized them, married them, and buried their relatives. They had a sort of family history together. As a result, it was possible for them to disagree with him on a single issue while still preserving their respect for him. Because there was already an established relationship, the issue did not become the relationship.

Reverend Lewis seems to have benefited from a similar situation in Charleston, West Virginia. On several occasions, the members of the Vestry of his church noted that they were unsure what they would do if presented with Lewis's moral choices. Because of their experience with Lewis, however, they were willing to trust him to make the right decision. This sort of trust takes time to build.

3. Whenever possible, a minister considering a controversial action should ask for the congregation's advice. This has two benefits: first, it forces the congregation to become involved in the debate, to educate themselves and study the issue; second, it shows respect for those members who may end up on the losing side or who disagree with the pastor's stand. That respect is the key to keeping them in the church. They must feel that their voice is still listened to—that while they may not have prevailed on this one issue, they are not being dismissed as irrelevant.

The best example of this is Mahan Siler's handling of Kevin and Steven's marriage request. Siler could easily have agreed to perform a private ceremony in a rented hall. It would have saved a lot of time and trouble for everyone involved, and Siler could have argued that he acted within his rights and personal conscience. And if the whole thing had remained a secret, Siler's job would have been a lot safer.

Such secrets rarely keep, however, and Siler might have found himself in the situation of Reverend Lewis, whose congregation found out that he had already performed two same-sex marriages. (Lewis had kept the ceremonies secret at the request of the couples involved.) That left some members of Lewis's congregation feeling hurt and betrayed. They had not been consulted, and it seemed as if Lewis didn't care what they thought.

By contrast, Siler went to the diaconate and explained what he wanted to do. He made no secret of his own position on the issue, but he did it in a way that showed he valued the views of his congregation. As he put it to them, "I wanted you to understand my position. But equally I want you to understand my respect for the wisdom of Pullen." That is the essence of what a minister should convey to his church.

A pastor who performs a controversial action—however right or wrong—without consulting his congregation will immediately polarize it into warring camps. The issue becomes the pastor himself, rather than the action. Those on the offended side will feel that their back is against the wall, and that no compromise is possible. They will believe that their feelings have been ignored, and they will be fighting to make those feelings heard. They will not be doing much listening.

By asking for advice or permission, a pastor creates the possibility for constructive dialogue. People *may* be able to talk for a while before their positions harden, and may even find it possible to "agree to disagree."

4. Try to get all parties to agree to the details of the decision-making process in advance, including how long the issue will be discussed, what sort of forums should be held, and exactly how the vote will be conducted. At both Pullen and Binkley, there was a bitter last-minute dispute over whether the vote should be done in person or by mail, and it led to hard feelings. The losing side will always claim that the issue hasn't been studied long enough, that they would surely win if it were studied a bit longer, and that the church leaders are manipulating the outcome by ending the discussion period. The church leaders need to be able to point to a document and say, "Look, we all agreed that this was the right amount of time to spend on this subject, and we're just sticking to the deadline."

5. Try to organize forums on the subject as a "search for the truth" or a "search for God's will" rather than as a debate. A debate is confrontational: it takes place between two sides, and one can only participate by choosing a side and fighting for it. Debates must have winners, and therefore losers. A search, in contrast, is something a group of people do together to arrive at a common goal.

Judy Purvis of Chapel Hill Friends was right to emphasize the need to "introduce this topic to the community in a way that gives people a chance to think about it without having to get rushed into a decision. Because when you rush people into a decision, if they're not comfortable with it, it tends to harden their position. You need to give them time, you need to give people space to explore how they feel, and how other people feel." Ideally, you want to give people a chance to talk and listen for as long as possible without forcing them to choose a position and defend it.

It's good to begin by having people talk about their feelings. Feelings aren't right or wrong. Let people talk about what makes them uncomfortable. Does the sight of two women kissing make them squirm? Does the thought of two men kissing make them feel even worse? Or do they sometimes feel unwelcome in their own church, that they are less of a member than a straight person is? Give people space to be uncomfortable and to get used to new ideas. Once the feelings are out in the open, it may be possible to separate intellectual discussions of Scripture and justice from gut reactions.

6. At every possible opportunity, remind one another of what binds you together as a community of faith. For example, you might begin each discussion of the subject by having the moderator state, "We are [denomination], brought together by our shared faith in [biblical inerrancy, Quaker process, the priesthood of the believer]." The point of this is to remind everyone involved that the church is bigger than this one issue. No matter what happens, those on both sides of the conflict will still have a place in the church when it is done. It is possible to "agree to disagree" on one issue, because we agree on more important ones.

Denominational Overview

Conflicts over homosexuality are simmering in a number of denominations:

Presbyterians. In 1978 the Presbyterian General Assembly voted to establish a church policy on homosexuality. The new policy was something of a compromise, attempting to recognize homosexuals as children of God while at the same time condemning homosexual behavior as "incompatible with Christian faith and life." The resolution had three essential components.

1. Everyone, including homosexuals, should be welcome in the Presbyterian church.
2. The Presbyterian church should work to abolish laws that discriminate against homosexuals.
3. The General Assembly offered "definitive guidance" against the ordination of "unrepentant, self-affirming, practicing homosexuals." A grandfather clause, however, would allow all gay and lesbian clergy ordained before 1978 to continue serving. In the Presbyterian denomination, church elders and deacons are considered ordained clergy. Thus this clause prevents homosexuals from serving in any leadership position within a congregation.

The 1978 policy represented a clear contradiction—in one breath condemning discrimination against homosexuals and in the next mandating such discrimination within the church itself. A group formed to protest the resolution almost immediately. Known as the "More Light" movement, it consists of Presbyterian churches that have signed a pledge to accept gay men and lesbians as full members of their congregations, including the privilege of holding office. At last count, there were approximately fifty More Light churches in the United States.

In 1985 the Permanent Judicial Commission of the General Assembly moved against the More Light Churches Network for violating the 1978 policy. The commission brought charges against Westminster Presbyterian Church of Buffalo, New York, for allowing gay men and lesbians to be deacons and elders. Westminster Church argued unsuccessfully that the 1978 policy was not binding on local churches and presbyteries, which have traditionally been allowed to make their own hiring decisions. Instead, the Permanent Judicial Commission ruled that the More Light pledge was illegal, and that any church signing it would be subject to disciplinary action. Over the next seven years, charges were filed against More Light churches in Oregon, Minnesota, and New York.

In 1988 the General Assembly commissioned a report examining the Presbyterian church's approach to sexuality. Three years in the making, the report was finally issued in 1991 under the title "Sexuality, Spirituality, and Social Justice." It quickly became the focus of controversy. The committee in charge of issuing the report had been unable to agree on a draft. The majority report called for a drastic rethinking of the church's stand on all aspects of human sexuality, and in particular homosexuality. After a close reading of Scripture and a study of the scientific data available, the majority report recommended that the church should treat homosexuals and their relationships with the same respect that it treats heterosexuals and theirs. This finding was unacceptable to several conservative members of the committee, who issued their own minority report. They too examined Scripture and scientific data, but found them to condemn homosexuality unequivocally as immoral and unhealthy. The General Assembly studied both reports. By an overwhelming margin of 501 to 7, the delegates voted to overrule the committee and accept the minority report. Presbyterian congregations were given until 1996 to study the report.

The conflict between conservative and More Light Presbyterians has only become more heated with the passage of time. (One well-publicized case arose in 1992 involving the Reverend Jane Spahr.[1]) In 1992 one California presbytery went so far as to ask the General Assembly to expel all gay men and lesbians from the Presbyterian church and send them to other denominations. At the 1994 General Assembly, a proposal was made to forbid any minister to perform same-sex unions. This measure was passed by the assembly, and is now being ratified by the presbyteries. It was expected to go into effect at the 1995 General Assembly.

The 1996 General Assembly will be the focus of particularly heated debate. That year marks the end of the study period on the divisive 1991 sexuality report. Several presbyteries will probably submit overtures to repeal the ban on gay and lesbian ministers. Given the current climate in the Presbyterian denomination, they are unlikely to succeed—yet.

Lutherans. The organization "Lutherans Concerned" was formed in 1974 to educate Lutherans about gay and lesbian issues and to work toward understanding and acceptance in that denomination. Like the More Light network among the Presbyterians, Lutherans Concerned encourages churches to adopt a policy of welcoming lesbians and gay men as full and equal members of their congregations. Churches that adopt such a policy are described as "Reconciled in Christ."

For many years the Lutheran church avoided a formal statement of its position on homosexuality. In 1989, however, the Evangelical Lutheran Church in America (ELCA, the largest Lutheran denomination) adopted a policy stating, "The Biblical understanding which this church affirms is that the normative setting for sexual intercourse is marriage. . . . Practicing homosexuals are excluded from the ordained ministry."

The new policy was immediately challenged by two of the ELCA's member churches: St. Francis Lutheran Church and First United Lutheran Church, both in San Francisco. One had called a gay man to be its pastor; the other had called a lesbian couple. The two churches were tried at a public hearing held in San Francisco in July of 1990. They were suspended from membership in the ELCA, and if they were still in violation of the policy at the end of 1995 they would be permanently removed from membership.[2]

In December of 1990, a seminary student named Bill Kunisch was preaching at his home church in Pigeon, Michigan. During his sermon, he mentioned that while at seminary in Berkeley, he had regularly attended worship services at St. Francis, and that he thought it was a good place, "pretty much like every other Lutheran Church I've ever been in." Kunisch went on to explain his feelings about that church, whose stand against the ELCA he supported: "I hesitate to talk about this because I realize the differences of opinion on homosexuality in the Church, and I think it's important for us to respect people whose opinions differ from our own. By talking about this I'm not trying to manipulate people into coming to the same conclusion I have come to. But I would urge you all to talk about it, study it, and listen to the stories of gay and lesbian people and continue to pray for the Holy Spirit as you come to your own conclusion about this issue."[3]

For making this statement, Kunisch was accused of being a homosexual by his church council, which terminated his financial aid, and by his Synod Candidacy Committee, which withdrew its endorsement for his ordination. He was forced to leave seminary. Seminary students staged several demonstrations across the country, protesting the Lutheran church's treatment of him.

Currently, the biggest controversy in the ELCA concerns its social statement on human sexuality. In 1993 the ELCA released a draft statement of the church's thinking about homosexuality. Like the Presbyterian majority report of 1991, it encouraged the church to view sexuality— including such taboo forms as masturbation and homosexuality—as a healthy part of human life. Unfortunately, the draft was leaked to the Associated Press before it could be released to the churches for study, and it became the subject of controversy before anyone had even read it. The ELCA leadership was the object of an onslaught of angry phone calls and hate mail—including several death threats.

The church leaders seem to have been shaken by the magnitude of the reaction against the statement. The original plan had been to give churches a few months to file comments on the draft, and then to begin work on revising it. Instead, the Division of Church and Society effectively fired the committee that had created the draft and appointed a new committee to compose a new social statement. The new statement was released in November of 1994. It is a pale reflection of the original and recommends few changes from traditional church teachings on sexuality. Congregations could file comments until the end of June 1995, when a report was to be presented at the ELCA's Biennial Churchwide Assembly. The final draft will be presented at the 1997 assembly.

United Church of Christ. The United Church of Christ ordained its first openly gay minister, Bill Johnson, in the 1970s. Since then, the General Synod has adopted a policy stating that homosexuality should not be a bar to ordination and encouraging local church associations to consider homosexual candidates for the ministry on the same terms as heterosexual candidates. The final decision on ordination policies has been left to the local associations, however, and not all of them have chosen to follow the General Synod's lead. Some associations, such as Western North Carolina, have gone to the other extreme, implementing policies which state that they will never consider a gay candidate for the ministry, regardless of his or her qualifications.

The General Synod has also encouraged its member churches to adopt policies barring discrimination against homosexuals in membership, employment, or volunteer services. Those churches that vote to adopt such a policy are referred to as "Open and Affirming" congregations.

Unitarian-Universalists. Unitarian-Universalists have long seen their affirmation of gay and lesbian rights as an essential component of their denomination's support for all human rights. The Unitarian-Universalist General Assembly passed its first resolution on the subject in 1970, on the first anniversary of the Stonewall riots. The resolution committed the denomination to work against laws regulating private consensual activity between adults, to oppose discrimination against homosexuals in the workplace, and to oppose discrimination by the U.S. government in the award of security clearances, visas, and citizenship.

Nineteen seventy-seven brought Anita Bryant and her campaign to paint gay men as dangerous child molesters. The UU General Assembly responded with a resolution calling on its members to fight negative propaganda against gay men and lesbians and to educate the public.

In 1984 the General Assembly passed a business resolution affirming the use of "services of union" to join same-sex couples.

In the 1990s, the denomination has repeatedly spoken out against campaigns by the religious right to restrict the rights of homosexuals. The General Assembly issued "Resolutions of Immediate Witness" against the antigay ballot initiatives in Oregon and Colorado and against the military's ban on homosexual soldiers. At its 1993 meeting in Charlotte, the General Assembly staged a public protest against North Carolina's sodomy laws. Also that year, the General Assembly formally endorsed the March on Washington for Lesbian, Gay, and Bisexual Equal Rights and Liberation.

Southern Baptists. In 1979 a fundamentalist was elected president of the Southern Baptist Convention for the first time, and he began appointing fellow fundamentalists to key positions. For the next ten years, the moderates and fundamentalists battled for power over the convention. The moderates, however, were never able to regain the presidency, and by 1989 the fundamentalists were in undisputed control.

Still firmly in power, the fundamentalists have shown no interest in compromise with the moderates. Indeed, they have continued to cement their position, reaching into lower and lower levels of the church hierarchy and evicting moderates from positions at Baptist colleges and universities. The 1992 expulsions of the Pullen and Binkley churches, as well as the new rule requiring all Southern Baptist churches to oppose homosexuality, were viewed by many moderates as an attempt by the fundamentalists to impose their dogma on individual congregations. With no real voice in the Southern Baptist Convention, the moderates have been forming their own organizations, such as the Cooperative Baptist Fellowship. In many ways, the Fellowship is now functioning as a proto-denomination, and it is likely that the moderates will formally split from the Southern Baptist Convention within the next ten years. The split will effectively resolve the issue of homosexuality for some time, placing the different camps in different denominations.

Methodists. The Methodists hold their General Conference every four years. At the 1984 conference, they adopted the statement that "no self-avowed practicing homosexual shall be ordained." At every conference since then, attempts have been made to repeal that statement. So far, however, none of the votes has come close to overturning it.

In 1992 the denomination released the results of a four-year study on homosexuality. The study covered the basic scientific and biblical issues in a nonjudgmental fashion, and has been described as a sort of "Homosexuality 101."[4] The report concluded with three recommendations. The first, that the study be circulated to Methodist churches for reading, was approved. So was the second, which added a stronger paragraph in support of gay and lesbian civil rights to the Methodist *Social Principles*. The last recommendation, however, was defeated. It would have changed the statement in the *Social Principles* that Methodists do not condone homosexuality to one saying, "We are not of a common mind about this."

Two major issues will probably dominate the 1996 General Conference. The first will be another attempt to repeal the ban on gay clergy, which is likely to be defeated. The second will be a new rule forbidding Methodist ministers from performing same-sex union ceremonies, and it is likely to pass.

Roman Catholics. For many years there has been a growing tension between the Italian and American branches of the Catholic church, particularly on issues of sexuality—contraception, premarital sex, and homosexuality. American Roman Catholics have, as a group, become somewhat more liberal on these issues, while the Italian branch and the pope have remained staunchly conservative. The gap will only get larger with time.

Although an actual split of the church is unlikely, it is difficult to see how this rift will be repaired in the near future. The election of a moderate pope who could span the two sides would probably make a significant difference. Given the makeup of the College of Cardinals, however, this event is unlikely.

Quakers. As we have seen, Quaker meetings are so independent that it is meaningless to talk of a denominational stand on the issue of homosexuality. Nonetheless, we may expect to see a steadily increasing number of nonprogrammed meetings performing same-sex marriages. Given the Quaker tradition of civil disobedience, I suspect that some of these marriages will be used as test cases attempting to introduce same-sex marriage into civil law.

The other branch of Quakers, Evangelical Friends, tends to be much more conservative. They are likely to follow whatever norms society eventually establishes about same-sex marriages rather than leading a fight to change them.

CHAPTER 3. *License to Preach*

The information in this chapter was obtained from the following sources. Interviews: John Blevins (January–April, 1992; October 1992), Olin Jolly (April 28, 1993), and Byron McCane (February 1992). Newspaper reportage: "Baptists Vote to Bar Gays," *Durham Herald-Sun*, June 10, 1992, pp. A1, A2; Kay McLain, "Pastors Say Autonomy in Question," *Durham Herald-Sun*, June 13, 1992, pp. 1B, 2B; "Sanctioning Gay Lives, Two Churches Feel Wrath," *New York Times*, May 2, 1992, p. Y11; Mark Schultz, "Pastor Backs Decision to Let Gay Member Preach," *Durham Herald-Sun*, February 22, 1992, p. B6; Mark Schultz, "Eye in a Storm of Controversy," *Durham Herald-Sun*, May 17, 1992, p. B5; Ruth Sheehan, "Binkley to Revisit Licensing Decision," *Raleigh News and Observer*, June 12, 1992, p. 3B. Letters to the editor, *Chapel Hill News*: Leslie Coggins, December 6, 1992; Bonnie Hensley, November 29, 1992; Paul Lindsay et al. (116 signees total), December 2, 1992; C. Douglas McFadyen, December 11, 1992; Lewis Miles, November 27, 1992; Shirley Finch Simons, December 6, 1992; Jerry Vansant, November 27, 1992. Other documents: *Binkley Newsletter*, March 31, 1992; John Blevins, "Who's in Charge Here?" sermon delivered at Olin T. Binkley Memorial Baptist Church, December 29, 1991; Jim and Dot Cansler, letter to the congregation of Olin T. Binkley Memorial Baptist Church, March 5, 1992; Diaconate of Olin T. Binkley Memorial Baptist Church, letter to the congregation, March 17, 1992; John L. Humber, "The Ordeal and Tragedy of Binkley Baptist Church," 1992; Richard Jenkins, letter to the congregation of Olin T. Binkley Memorial Baptist Church, February 15, 1992; Olin Jolley, open letter to the congregation of Olin T. Binkley Memorial Baptist Church; resolution adopted by Olin T. Binkley Memorial Baptist Church, April 5, 1992. Selected items in information packet distributed to the members of Olin T. Binkley Memorial Baptist Church: Byron McCane, "On the Ordination of Homosexuals"; Robert Seymour, "The Church and Homosexuality"; Jim Wells, letter.

1. John Blevins, "Who's in Charge Here?" sermon delivered at Olin T. Binkley Memorial Baptist Church, December 29, 1991.

2. Byron McCane, brief interview, February 1992. My experience with McCane epitomizes the difficulty I had in interviewing those on the conservative side in churches' conflicts over homosexuality. He was unwilling, in fact, even to tell me which side of the debate he was on, saying it was a private matter. When I asked him if he had left Binkley because of the discussion of John's licensure—something I knew he had told other members of the congregation—he answered that such a statement would be an "exaggeration to the point of being untrue."

3. Byron McCane, "On the Ordination of Homosexuals," in information packet distributed to the members of Olin T. Binkley Memorial Baptist Church.

4. Ibid.

5. Ibid.

6. Richard Jenkins, letter to the congregation of Olin T. Binkley Memorial Baptist Church, February 15, 1992. Quoted in John L. Humber, "The Ordeal and Tragedy of Binkley Baptist Church," 1992, p. 27.

7. Diaconate of Olin T. Binkley Memorial Baptist Church, letter to the congregation, March 17, 1992.

8. Reported in John L. Humber, "The Ordeal and Tragedy of Binkley Baptist Church," 1992, p. 41.

9. Ibid., p. 45.

10. Leslie Coggins, letter to the editor, *Chapel Hill News*, December 6, 1992.

11. John L. Humber, "The Ordeal and Tragedy of Binkley Baptist Church," 1992, pp. 56, 59.

12. Ibid., p. 59.

13. There were a number of reasons for Jordon's forced resignation, not all of them having to do with the licensure conflict. There were many conservatives who had never approved of a woman minister in the first place. There were also personal conflicts. The licensure debate, nevertheless, was the single most important factor. Interestingly, it seems to have cost her support on both sides of the struggle.

The same was true of a rumor that circulated through the church alleging that Jordan was a lesbian. For the conservatives, this rumor confirmed their belief that Jordan had somehow manipulated the process to her own political ends. To the liberals, this rumor made Jordan seem a hypocrite, since she had not "come out of the closet" to support the licensure.

CHAPTER 4   *The Class of 1992*

Information in this chapter was obtained from the following sources. Interviews: Richard Bardusch (1992; October 4, 1993), John Blevins (October 9, 1993), the Reverend H. Joanne Stearns, and Paul Wessinger (February 21, 1993). Newspaper reportage: David Folkenflik, "Duke Student Fakes Cancer," *Durham Herald-Sun*, April 16, 1993, pp. A1, A6; Michael Saul, "Divinity Student Allegedly Bilked Funds," *Chronicle* (Duke University), vol. 88, no. 134, April 19, 1993, pp. 1, 16. Letters to the editor, *Between Times* (Duke Divinity School): Richard Bardusch, October 11, 1990; John Blevins, "Letter to the Divinity School Community," December 12, 1990; Mary McClintok Fulkerson, October 11, 1990; Jeremy Howell, October 2, 1990; Charles Stanford, October 11, 1990; Jack D. Wallace, Jr., October 24, 1990. Other documents: Divinity School Students for Gay and Lesbian Concerns, minutes, academic year 1990–91; Divinity School Students for Gay and Lesbian Concerns, Steering Committee, letter to Dr. Richard B. Hays, September 16, 1991; Duke University Task Force on Gay, Lesbian, and Bisexual Matters, *1991–1992 Report*, August 28, 1992; Richard B. Hays, letter to the Steering Committee of Divinity School Students for Gay and Lesbian Concerns, September 21, 1991; posters hung around Duke Divinity School, fall 1990.

1. Mary McClintok Fulkerson, letter to the editor, *Between Times* (Duke Divinity School), October 11, 1990.

2. Jack D. Wallace, Jr., letter to the editor, *Between Times* (Duke Divinity School), October 11, 1990.

3. David Folkenflik, "Duke Student Fakes Cancer," *Durham Herald-Sun*, April 16, 1993, pp. A1, A6; see also Michael Saul, "Divinity Student Allegedly Bilked Funds," *Chronicle* (Duke University), vol. 88, no. 134, April 19, 1993, pp. 1, 16.

CHAPTER 5   *The Long-Term Cost*

Information in this chapter was obtained from the following sources. Interview: with Jim Lewis (March 30, 1993). Newspaper reportage: Ruth Jones, "Lewis Ostracized for Stand," *Charleston Daily Mail*, May 25, 1977; Bob Kittle, "Special Meeting Called: Lewis's Action Stirs Episcopalians," *Charleston Daily Mail*, 1977; "Priest Backs Down," *Front Page* (Raleigh), May 13, 1994, p. 1; Tom Riesenberg, "Gays Relieved by Decision on Lewis," *Charleston Gazette*, June 2, 1977, p. 3A; John Scruggs, "Lewis Risks All for Gays," *Front Page* (Raleigh), April 29, 1994, pp. 1, 24. Other documents: Jim Lewis, Statement to St. John's Episcopal Church, May 31, 1977.

1. Jim Lewis, Statement to St. John's Episcopal Church, May 31, 1977.
2. Ibid.
3. Ibid.
4. Ibid.
5. Ibid.
6. Ibid.
7. Ibid.
8. Tom Riesenberg, "Gays Relieved by Decision on Lewis," *Charleston Gazette*, June 2, 1977, p. 3A.

CHAPTER 6 *A Place to Meet*

The information in this chapter was obtained from the following sources. Interviews: Geraldine Bryan (December 14, 1992), Jimmy Creech (July 30, 1993), Carolyn King (January 6, 1993), Syh King (January 6, 1993), Wayne Lindsey (January 26, 1993), June Norris (February 1, 1993), Cally Rodgers-Witte (November 30, 1992), Clay Stalnaker (February 16, 1993), and Willie J. White (February 25, 1993). Documents: Community United Church of Christ, minutes of Church Council meeting, March 27, 1977; Community United Church of Christ, minutes of Called Congregational Meeting, April 17, 1977; Community United Church of Christ, minutes of Annual Congregational Meeting, December 17, 1989; June Norris, letter to the author, received March 8, 1995; Rufus H. Stark, letter to the editor, *Raleigh News and Observer*, February 17, 1979, p. 4.

1. Admittedly, this is an odd detail, taken from my interview with Reverend White. Unfortunately, no one else I've spoken with knows anything about Sister Evelyn, and I have been unable to locate her for an interview.

2. Ironically, the Raleigh Religious Network for Gay and Lesbian Equality now meets in that same student lounge from time to time. The current Session has made no complaint about their presence.

3. Rufus H. Stark, letter to the editor, *Raleigh News and Observer*, February 17, 1979, p. 4.

4. No relation to June Norris.

5. See, for example, John J. McNeill, *Taking a Chance on God* (Boston: Beacon Press, 1989).

6. After reading this quote, Norris wrote me in March 1995 to say that she still disagrees with Lindsey on what the conflict was all about:

> If that's what people were "hearing" in ALL my sermons, I wonder if they were "listening." During Lent I worked on "Christian growth." I've listened to *many* tapes and I think the idea of "It's OK to be gay and Christian" sermon criticisms was a smoke screen.

Write it as you see fit. Wayne knows what the beef was. They didn't tell *ME* that!

CHAPTER 7 *The Quaker Process*

The information in this chapter was obtained from the following sources. Interviews: Bill Flash (February 3, 1993), Elisa Jones (February 3, 1993), Judy Purvis (November 18, 1992), Anne Riggs (February 13, 1993), Roxanne Seagraves (August 3, 1992), and Cris South (February 5, 1993). Documents: Chapel Hill Friends Meeting, "Marriage under the Care of the Meeting," undated; Joe Dipierro, "Memo to the Overseers," November 10, 1990; Bruce Grimes, "Religious Society of Friends Inclusive Minutes on Marriage," Friends for Gay and Lesbian Concerns, undated; Steve Phillips, "Memorandum to the Committee on Ministry and Worship of Chapel Hill Friends Meeting," December 16, 1990; Roxanne Seagraves, letter to the author, February 22, 1995.

1. Bruce Grimes, "Religious Society of Friends Inclusive Minutes on Marriage," Friends for Gay and Lesbian Concerns, undated.

CHAPTER 8 *A Challenge for the Process*

The information in this chapter was obtained from the following sources. Interviews: Gary Briggs (November 2, 1993), Jim Gilkeson (August 7, 1993), John Hunter (January 30, 1993), Don Markle (February 5, 1993), Bob Passmore, Cornelia Sparks (February 19, 1993), and Sue Unrue (October 28, 1993). Durham Friends Meeting documents: newsletter, First Month, Second Month, 1993; "Notes from a brief forum regarding marriage at Durham Friends Meeting," June 28, 1992; "Procedures for Marriage in Durham Monthly Meeting of the Religious Society of Friends," June 29, 1993; "Queries on Same-Sex Marriage," October 7, 1990; "Summary of Perspectives from the Discussion on Marriage Process Options of 16 April 1993"; "What Do Friends Mean by Marriage?—A discussion among members and attenders of Durham Friends Meeting, January 20, 1993"; Ministry and Counsel Committee, letter to Jim Gilkeson, May 13, 1992. Other documents: Cal and Virgie Geiger, "'What Is Marriage,' as We Understand It," undated letter to Durham Friends Meeting; Jim Gilkeson, letter to Kathleen March and the Committee on Ministry and Counsel, April 30, 1992; Jim Gilkeson, "Quakers and Marriage—Some Personal Thoughts," January 14, 1993; Mary Harwood, letter to those at the discussion session taking place January 20, 1993; John Hunter, "Marriage Is . . . —Statements for Discussion," January 1993; John Hunter, "Marriage under the Care of the Durham Meeting—Some Thoughts and Questions by John Hunter," undated; John Hunter, "The Relationship of the Meeting to Couples Married under Its Care," undated; Ned Kennington, "Some Thoughts on the Definition of Marriage," January 16, 1993; Don Markle, letter to the author, February 26, 1995; Don Markle, proposed minute for Durham Friends Meeting, undated.

1. Durham Friends Meeting, "Queries on Same-Sex Marriage," October 7, 1990.

2. Jim Gilkeson, letter to Kathleen March and the Committee on Ministry and Counsel, April 30, 1992.

3. Not from the original letter but described by Don Markle in letter to the author, February 26, 1995.

4. Interview, Don Markle, February 5, 1993. Clarification from Markle, letter to the author, February 26, 1995.

CHAPTER 9 *Race, the Vatican, and Inclusiveness*

The information in this chapter was obtained from the following sources. Interviews: Bruce Bavinger (September 1, 1993), Mike Baxter (February 25, 1993), Janet Jezsik (March 7, 1993), Kevin Calegari (March 5, 1993), David Kirkpatrick (April 15, 1993), and Thomas Sherratt (February 26, 1993; February 12, 1995). News reportage: "Return to Sender," *Dignity/USA Journal*, vol. 24, no. 4, Fall 1992, pp. 4, 5. Other documents: Congregation for the Doctrine of the Faith, "Declaration on Certain Questions Concerning Sexual Ethics" (1975), "Letter to the Bishops of the Catholic Church on the Pastoral Care of Homosexual Persons" (1986), "Some Considerations Concerning the Catholic Response to Legislative Proposals on the Non-Discrimination of Homosexual Persons" (1992).

In researching the case of Holy Cross, I discovered that not one member of the church's black leadership was willing to talk to me. I did find some other members who were willing to chat with me off the record, however. And by comparing my interviews with Bruce Bavinger and Janet Jezsik, I could work out a fairly objective picture of what was said at the relevant Parish Council meetings. But I still needed to know why it had been said. What had the Parish Council been thinking? What had motivated it to take the action it did? In the end I had to settle for a second-best solution. Shortly after Dignity was expelled, a white church member named David Kirkpatrick was appointed to the Parish Council. The leadership was willing to answer David's questions about the meetings, and he was willing to answer mine. Such secondhand information is always a little suspect, and I would have preferred an on-the-record interview with the leaders themselves—but I accepted what I could get. Kirkpatrick's account agrees substantially with Father Bavinger's descriptions of the council's positions, providing a reasonably accurate picture.

Epigraph: Frederick Millen, Commentary, *Dignity/USA Journal*, vol. 24, no. 4, Fall 1992, p. 6.

1. Congregation for the Doctrine of the Faith, "Letter to the Bishops of the Catholic Church on the Pastoral Care of Homosexual Persons" (1986). In *Origins: NC Documentary Service*, November 13, 1986, vol. 16, no. 22, pp. 1, 379–382.

2. Dignity USA, "Our History—Where We've Come From," undated, p. 2.

3. Congregation for the Doctrine of the Faith, "Some Considerations Concerning the Catholic Response to Legislative Proposals on the Non-Discrimination of Homosexual Persons" (1992). Reprinted in *Dignity/USA Journal*, vol. 24, no. 4, Fall 1992, p. 14.

Denominational Overview

The information in this appendix was obtained from the following sources. Interviews: Mark Bowman (March 3, 1995), Bonnie Crouse (June 10, 1994, and correspondence), Bob Gibeling (March 3, 1995), John Graves (March 30, 1993), Joe Harvard (March 23, 1993), Morris Hundgins (November 4, 1992), Ken Marks (January 12, 1993; May 7, 1994), and Allan Proctor (January 14, 1993; May 9, 1994). Documents: Lutherans Concerned, "Homophobia in the ELCA: The Case of Seminarian Bill Kunisch"; Presbyterians for Gay and Lesbian Concerns, *More Light Update*, October 1992; Jane Spahr, "Answering the Call: Commitment, Work, and Worship," *Christianity and Crisis*, January 4, 1993, p. 423; Special Committee on Human Sexuality, *Majority Report to the 203rd General Assembly of the Presbyterian Church*, 1991; Special Committee on Human Sexuality, *Minority Report to the 203rd General Assembly of the Presbyterian Church*, 1991.

1. The year 1992 brought one of the most heavily publicized conflicts within the Presbyterian church. The Downtown United Church of Rochester, New York, had called Jane Spahr to serve as its pastor. Although an open lesbian, Spahr had been ordained before the 1978 resolution, and thus was eligible to serve under the grandfather clause. Her call was upheld by the Genessee Valley Presbytery, which oversees the Downtown United Church, and by the synod that oversees the presbytery. Nonetheless, the Permanent Judicial Commission of the General Assembly chose to prosecute the church for its choice of pastor. After hearing the case, it ordered that Spahr's call be set aside—in essence saying that she could not serve as a minister even though the congregation of Downtown United Church wanted her to. Downtown United Church eventually outmaneuvered the Permanent Judicial Commission on a technicality, hiring Spahr for the position of "Evangelist" rather than pastor.

2. Although St. Francis and First United are almost certain to be expelled from the denomination on January 1, 1996, the two churches have enjoyed a measure of support in their own area. In 1993 the Sierra-Pacific Synod, to which the churches belong, passed a resolution stating that it will continue to "maintain a strong bond of fellowship" with the two churches even after they are expelled. In addition, one of the gay ministers, Jeff Johnson, was elected by his fellow pastors to be dean of his local "cluster" of churches.

In nearby Oakland, Ross Merkel, the pastor of St. Paul's Lutheran Church, came out of the closet in 1993. He also announced that he was living in a committed relationship with another man. The ELCA held a disciplinary hearing and removed Merkel from the clergy roster, making him ineligible to serve at a Lutheran church. The congregation of St. Paul's decided to defy the ELCA leadership, however, and retained Merkel as their pastor anyway. The new bishop for the synod, Robert Matthias, has since bent over backward to avoid expelling St. Paul's from the ELCA. In a letter of January 1995 he described the ministerial position at St. Paul's as open—rather than admitting that the church has a gay pastor, he is simply taking the view that it hasn't gotten around to hiring one at all.

3. The quotes from Kunisch's sermon are as reported in a pamphlet, "Homophobia in the ELCA: The Case of Seminarian Bill Kunisch," available through Lutherans Concerned.

4. Mark Bowman, interview, March 3, 1995.

Index

About the Author

Keith Hartman was born in Huntsville, Alabama. He graduated from Princeton University in 1988, and pursued graduate studies at the London School of Economics and Duke University. In 1993 he made the pleasant discovery that he could make a living as a writer—well, sort of a living, anyway—and ran away from his Ph.D. program. He has (among other things) worked as a theater and dance critic, covered the story of a marine who went on a shooting spree while chanting "Clinton must pay," interviewed a black lesbian medical student about the surprising attitudes toward race, sexuality, and AIDS in the tribal homelands of South Africa, and written a series of columns under the title "Sex, God, etc."